The APPELLATE PROSECUTOR

A PRACTICAL
AND INSPIRATIONAL GUIDE
TO APPELLATE ADVOCACY

Edited by
Ronald H. Clark
Adjunct Professor,
Seattle University Law School

Order this book online at www.trafford.com
or email orders@trafford.com

Most Trafford titles are also available at major online book retailers.

© Copyright 2005 Ronald H. Clark.
All rights reserved. No part of this publication may be reproduced,
stored in a retrieval system, or transmitted, in any form or by
any means, electronic, mechanical, photocopying, recording, or
otherwise, without the written prior permission of the author.

Cover photograph of Supreme Court Chamber by Franz
Jantzen and printed here courtesy of the Office of the Curator,
Supreme Court of the United States. Chapters 2 and 3 used
in this publication by permission of J. Frederic Voros, Jr.

Print information available on the last page.

ISBN: 978-1-4120-5130-9 (sc)

Because of the dynamic nature of the Internet, any web addresses or
links contained in this book may have changed since publication and
may no longer be valid. The views expressed in this work are solely those
of the author and do not necessarily reflect the views of the publisher,
and the publisher hereby disclaims any responsibility for them.

Any people depicted in stock imagery provided by Getty Images are
models, and such images are being used for illustrative purposes only.
Certain stock imagery © Getty Images.

Trafford rev. 01/30/2019

 www.trafford.com

North America & international
toll-free: 1 888 232 4444 (USA & Canada)
fax: 812 355 4082

CONTENTS

FOREWORD /   5
Charles E. Moylan, Jr.

ONE /   9
Persuasion, Planning and Analysis for Appellate Advocacy
Robert J. Humphreys

TWO /   25
Writing the Brief
J. Frederic Voros, Jr.

THREE /   51
Sample Appellate Brief Template
J. Frederic Voros, Jr.

FOUR /   59
Short Declarative Sentences: The Key To Good Legal Writing
Paul Turner

FIVE /   65
Writing the Persuasive Brief: (And Some Matters of Style)
Timothy A. Baughman

SIX /   80
Appellate Strategies
Robert M. Foster

SEVEN   95
Research Resources: An Appellate Lawyer's Tools of the Trade
Donald J. Zelenka

EIGHT /   115
Standards of Review: The First Line of Defense
James F. Flanagan

NINE / 131
Protecting the Record for Appeal: Advice for the Trial Prosecutor
J. Kirk Brown

TEN / 137
Professional Responsibility on Appeal
Barbara P. Hervey

ELEVEN / 148
How Appealing Is Your Case? Eight Considerations That May Influence a Decision to Appeal
Hilary L. Brunell

TWELVE / 157
Successful Appellate Oral Advocacy
Timothy A. Baughman

THIRTEEN / 168
Taking Advantage of Oral Argument
Kaye G. Hearn

FOURTEEN / 174
Decision Making: Conferencing of Cases
Jerry G. Elliott

FIFTEEN / 177
Judicial Conferencing in Appellate Courts
Nathan D. Mihara

SIXTEEN / 183
Fielding Difficult Questions From the Bench
Paul H. Anderson

SEVENTEEN / 197
Inspirational Words for the Appellate Prosecutor
Donald J. Zelenka

ACKNOWLEDGEMENTS 211

THE AUTHORS 213

FOREWORD

ODE TO A WATERBUG

He fascinates the human race,
By gliding o'er the water's face,
With ease, celerity and grace;
But if he ever stopped to think,
Of how he does it, he would sink.

Among lawyers, even among appellate prosecutors, such waterbugs are rare. There will, to be sure, be occasional prodigies—a Wolfgang Amadeus Mozart or a Shoeless Joe Jackson—who seem from birth to be destined for the Hall of Fame without conscious effort. This book is not for them. They are, in any event, a very niche market. For every such "natural," however, there are the countless students of their crafts—including already gifted rarities such as a Ted Williams or a Johann Sebastian Bach, an Emily Dickinson or a Peyton Manning—who do not hesitate to watch and to learn and to spend hours poring over the game films in order to perfect already significant talents and to reach beyond what might seem destined. This book is for them.

For a number of years, Editor Ron Clark organized and presided over a series of week-long seminars for appellate prosecutors under the sponsorship of the National College of District Attorneys. I had the honor of joining him on one such occasion. Ron brought together a galaxy of stars from every pertinent constituency and point of view—the ranks of the working prosecutor, the academic grove, attorney generals' offices, and the appellate bench. The appeals process was examined inside and out and from every possible angle. As an arithmetic inevitability, however, the number of appellate prosecutors who could manage a weeklong trip to Columbia, South Carolina was austerely limited.

Ron has now prevailed upon many of the stars who made up that galaxy to distill, and further to elaborate upon, their collective wisdom in written form for a far wider audience and in a more permanent format. This work in my judgment will find an indispensable place on the desk, or at the bedside on the night before argument, of every successful appellate prosecutor.

The book's coverage is plenary—the appellate brief, the appellate argument, and the strategic planning that should precede either brief or argument. That strategic planning, as Judge Bob Humphreys points out, should begin with a grasp of Aristotle's *Rhetoric* and the value of knowing your audience: "Know thy appellate judges." As a 34-year veteran of the appellate judging process, I especially empathize with Bob's view of the simple statement of facts. Any lawyer who can leave the legalese in the library and write a clean and engaging narrative has earned our sympathetic ear for whatever else he or she may have to say.

Hilary Brunell has supplied a thoughtful analysis of the frequently neglected subject of an appeal, in certain limited cases, taken by the prosecution. It is here that the prosecutor's office controls the strategy and the wise strategy should be, "Don't push a loser." It is better quietly to accept the loss of a battle, which may be little noticed, than to lose the war through an appellate decision that will be universally noticed.

I particularly enjoyed Bob Foster's ideas on how appellate prosecutors should study the personalities and the doctrinal predilections of both courts institutionally and judges individually. Courts and judges, consciously and subconsciously, have agendas and how a particular argument fits in with or conflicts with such agendas may be critical to the outcome of a case. Appellate lawyers need to know these agendas. Bob also makes the point that an advocate must be protective not only of his or her individual long-term credibility but also that of the office generally that he or she represents.

Veteran prosecutorial advocates Fred Voros and Tim Baughman and Justice Paul Turner focus different but insightful lenses on the art of writing effective and persuasive appellate briefs. Don Zelenka concisely pulls together the research resources that are the indispensable tools of the trade.

For the prosecutorial switch-hitter who must appear in the trial court and the appellate court alike, it is sometimes disconcerting to switch from selling a product to a market of lay jurors to the more monastic standards of appellate review. Professor Jim Flanagan provides a brilliant chapter on the at-times overlooked subject of those very special standards. Nebraska Solicitor General Kirk Brown carries the preparation responsibilities one step further back in pointing out that the appellate advocate is completely dependent on the extent to which the trial advocate has had the foresight to anticipate an appeal and to protect and preserve the record accordingly.

Judges Mike Keasler and Barbara Hervey, both of the Texas Court of Criminal Appeals, have provided an invaluable chapter on the special professional and ethical responsibilities that are imposed upon the appellate prosecutor above and beyond those that apply to appellate lawyers in general.

Even after the arts of appellate brief writing have been mastered, the forensic exercise of oral argument remains an art unto itself. Tim Baughman and Chief Judge Kaye Hearn both explore the subtleties of this very special craft in enlightening detail. These two chapters are "must" reading for any appellate prosecutor.

The goal, of course, of both the appellate brief and the appellate argument is to persuade an appellate court of the rightness of one's cause. Judge Jerry Elliott of the Kansas Court of Appeals, Justice Nathan Mihara of the California Court of Appeal, and Justice Paul Anderson of the Minnesota Supreme Court give us the insider's view of what goes on in the privacy of the conferencing room and what the factors are that sometimes turn the tide.

To this invaluable work on the art of appellate advocacy on behalf of the prosecution, Don Zelenka has appended a fitting denouement with his chapter on "Inspirational Words for the Appellate Advocate."

This book on the special skills of *The Appellate Prosecutor* fills a gaping need that had not heretofore been met. Appellate prosecutors throughout the land, who will be its beneficiaries, owe a debt of gratitude to the fourteen judges, professors, and veteran appellate lawyers who have pooled their talents and insights to fill this need and to Ron Clark for masterminding such a unique pooling of talent.

Charles E. Moylan, Jr.
Retired Judge
Maryland Court of Special Appeals

ONE

PERSUASION, PLANNING AND ANALYSIS FOR APPELLATE ADVOCACY

ROBERT J. HUMPHREYS
JUDGE, VIRGINIA COURT OF APPEALS
VIRGINIA BEACH, VIRGINIA

Judges are a lot like dogs. Individually, they can be friendly, agreeable, and dependable but beware when they travel in packs.

Judge Richard Posner, United States Court of Appeals for the Seventh Circuit.

You are standing in a room with thirty-foot ceilings, crystal chandeliers and the seal of your state or the United States over a long raised bench. With your peripheral vision you may note the legal themed murals or portraits of dead judges covering the walls. You gaze up at, not one, but a veritable pack of black-robed and stern-faced men and women. If it hasn't sunk in before now, you realize that you are about to engage in the ultimate exercise of skill in your chosen profession. Your written and spoken words on behalf of the client you are there to represent may make, alter or erase the law in the particular area at issue. Is it any wonder that most lawyers consider appellate litigation the most intimidating aspect of the practice of law?

The appeals' process is basically another manifestation of our adversary system of justice and should be approached as such. A particularly apt medical analogy is that if trial work is likened to surgery—appellate litigation is an autopsy. Both procedures involve many of the same tools, knowledge and skills, but one is devoted to determining what, if anything, went wrong with the other.

Like the trial prosecutor, the job of the appellate prosecutor is to persuade a neutral audience that the rule of law and perhaps even the abstract concept of justice compel a particular result. However, obvious differences exist between the trial and appellate processes as well. First, the audience you will work to persuade will be trained lawyers, instead of a lay jury. Second, the rules governing your appellate contest will be different. Nevertheless, the appeal, like the trial, is an adversarial battle that will be joined in a courtroom. To carry the military analogy a little further, it is a battle that will require intelligence, planning and analysis. You will need to know precisely what weapons you have to fight with (the facts of your case and the applicable law) and you will need to analyze the terrain in which your battle will be fought (the judges and procedural rules of the court that will decide the victor).

Stripped to its essence, an appellate court is simply another arena in which you and your opponent are given an equal opportunity to persuade an audience. If you are persuasive enough, you will win. If you accept that premise, then it logically follows that the process of persuasion is worthy of study. Indeed, an investment of time and effort in analyzing and planning how to best persuade your audience, under a given set of circumstances, will pay dividends—especially if your opponent does not make a similar investment of time and effort. The focus of this chapter is an analysis of the process of persuasion both generally and how that process applies specifically to appellate practice.

THE BASIC BUILDING BLOCKS OF PERSUASION

What you don't know will always hurt you.

First Law of Blissful Ignorance

Before we can get specific about the persuasion process in an appellate context, we probably should go over some basic elements of effective persuasion. These elements provide the foundation for every effective persuasive technique. This is the case whether you are preparing an appeal, trying a case to a jury, selling Girl Scout cookies or convincing the public to elect you to office.

> It is safe to assume legal doctrines that claim to be the offspring of logic are either not proud of, or not aware of, their real parents.
>
> *Felix S. Cohen, Attorney and Legal Scholar.*

1. "It's All Greek To Me!"

Over 2300 years ago, the Greek philosopher, Aristotle, laid the groundwork for modern public communication in a three-part work simply entitled "Rhetoric." Aristotle defined "rhetoric" as a branch of discourse centering on persuasion. In Aristotle's time, rhetoric was considered one of the two primary forms of expression. The word comes from the Greek "rhetor," meaning "speaker in an assembly" and concerned the practice of oratory, or formal public speaking. Rhetoric, as an avocation, may have started in the 5th century B.C. in response to citizens' need for help in pleading their own cases in court for the restoration of their property, which had been confiscated by the tyrant Thrasybulus (and so was born the trial lawyer).

Aristotle's teacher, Plato, hated the way that public speakers skillfully manipulated audiences with no apparent regard for truth. Plato saw little value in the type of rhetoric used by the fast-talking speakers of his day. However, his student Aristotle saw great potential in rhetoric (the dynamics of one person addressing many). He believed it was an art form that could and should be studied, and he proceeded to do so. Aristotle viewed the essence of the art of rhetoric as the ability to discern and make use of the most effective means of persuasion in a particular case. He asserted in his book that all effective public presentations are some ratio of three rhetorical vehicles: *ethos, pathos* and *logos.*

Essentially, the *ethos* component of rhetoric is the perception of the speaker's character as revealed through the speaker's communication, or the past experience of the audience with the speaker. The *pathos* element represents the emotions felt by the audience during the communication.

Finally, the *logos* aspect of rhetoric is the persuasive effect of the actual words used by the speaker.

Of the three components of rhetoric, Aristotle regarded *ethos* as the single most important element in the persuasive process. *Ethos* is more than simply your credibility as a messenger although that is certainly part of it. It is the speaker's reputation for credibility with the audience that is important. The more credible the audience perceives the speaker to be, the more credible the argument. If you take a moment to think about it, you form quite a few of your opinions based upon the level of trust you have in the person who is conveying the information upon which your opinion will be based.

Although no presenter today would speak without considering the audience, Aristotle's assertion of the importance of *pathos* was a novel idea in his time. He provides the earliest record of a rhetorician identifying the audience and their emotional reaction as an important part of public speaking. In fact, he believed that a speech was effective only if it stirred up emotions in its audience. In modern parlance, *pathos* is simply your ability to make use of any human values in your case in a way that your audience can either sympathize with or empathize with. The reality is that appellate judges are human and will find it much easier to apply the law if the result will also comport with their sense of justice.

The last element of rhetoric, but unfortunately the only one seriously considered by most appellate lawyers, is *logos* or the logical appeal of your message. *Logos* is simply the power of the syllogism. You remember what a syllogism is, don't you? All right, by way of a refresher, here is the classic example of a syllogism:

All men are mortal.
Aristotle is a man.
Therefore, Aristotle is mortal.

Or in a legal context:

A binding contract must be supported by consideration.
The agreement between Tom and Mary was not supported by consideration.
Therefore, no binding contract existed between Tom and Mary.

Whether as simplistic as the one noted or more complex, ideally, the logic of your argument is inexorable and compelling because you have demonstrated to your audience that, under the standard of review, the statutes of your jurisdiction, and the applicable precedent, your interpretation of the law is the only outcome that makes any sense.

So far, we have focused on the basic persuasive elements you, as the communicator, must master to be effective but up to this point we have left out of the equation the manner in which your audience will process your deathless prose and spellbinding oratory. It is time to remedy that deficiency.

2. The Thinking Process And Persuasion

> To learn from your mistakes, you first must realize that you are making mistakes.
>
> *Philo's Law*

Let us start with this simple proposition:

> *Attitudes drive behavior. If you can change attitudes, you influence behavior.*

Unlike the jury selection process available to the trial practitioner, in appellate practice you have little or no control over who your audience is going to be, but it would certainly be nice to know a bit about the people who will weigh your arguments. Who are those folks beneath the black robes? What kind of life experiences have they had? What is their judicial philosophy? What are their hot buttons and do I want to push them or not? What will their analytical process involve? In the course of a career of practice before these judges, you may come to learn the answers to many of these questions. However, it is the answer to the last question that may be the most important in determining how to persuade them.

Human beings think in basically one of two ways or modes: systemic mode and heuristic mode. Systemic mode thinking is characterized by a careful, deliberate and analytical approach to sifting information. The mind is active. The thinker is alert and more inclined to be process oriented with reason dominating over emotion.

By contrast, heuristic mode thinking reflects a stream-of-consciousness approach where the information is skimmed rather than critically analyzed. In this mode, the thinker is less likely to notice inconsistencies, factual errors and logical flaws. The thinker is not alert and inclined to be result oriented with emotion dominating over reason.

While one mode of thinking will tend to predominate over the other in all of us, we are all capable of thinking in both modes and we can and do switch between them. What this means in the context of appellate advocacy is that your persuasive efforts will have differing effects depending on the mode of thinking of your audience at the time your brief is read or your oral argument heard.

The thinking mode of the audience will not affect their perception of the credibility of the speaker or lack thereof (*ethos*), but it will affect the degree to which your audience will rely on your reputation for credibility to determine the outcome. Heuristic mode thinkers will rely more on your reputation for competence and professionalism than the systemic mode thinker, who is more likely to validate your analysis with their own. However, in general terms, an appeal based upon cold facts and logical reasoning is more likely to succeed with systemic mode thinkers (Aristotle's *logos* component) while an emotional appeal will likely be more successful with a heuristic mode thinker (you guessed it, *pathos*).

For example, if the decision to be made is whether or not to buy a new pair of sneakers, the question foremost in the mind of the systemic mode thinker might be: "How much do these sneakers cost?" In contrast, the big question for the heuristic mode thinker is more likely to be: "Does Michael Jordan endorse these sneakers?"

The problem you have as an appellate prosecutor is that you will not know whether your masterpiece of a brief will be read by a judge right after the judge has had their morning coffee on a day when all is right with the world or will it be read it at the end of a long day when that judge is tired, perhaps preoccupied with how to craft an opinion in another case or frustrated by a really bad brief that the judge finished reading just before picking up yours. Because there is no way to know the thinking modes of those in your audience at any particular point in time and assuming your position is not frivolous, you obviously will have to craft an approach that effectively deals with both modes of thinking.

So, how do you deal with an audience that is thinking in mixed modes? Well, like Joe Friday in the old Dragnet television series, systemic mode thinkers focus on "just the facts" and law important to resolving the legal issue. To appeal to those thinking in systemic mode, a well-written statement of facts and a well-organized brief will be key to assisting process-oriented thinkers. So, start by reminding the court of the standard of review, then apply the facts in an organized way consistent with the standard of review to the legal principles involved. At that point, if necessary, argue logical extensions of existing law to apply to those facts.

For any result-oriented heuristic thinkers, emphasize the human values in your statement of facts and use cues.[1] Remember, heuristic thinkers are looking for shortcuts to the bottom line so give them some. That is what cues are—shortcuts.

There are three cues or shortcuts that are particularly effective with heuristic thinkers in an appellate context: the *comparison cue,* the *liking cue* and the *authority cue.*

Have you ever wondered why television sitcoms use laugh tracks? When the laugh track is played, the studio audience assumes that what just happened is funny and laughs along (without any critical analysis about whether it actually was funny). The laugh track is simply the application of the *comparison cue,* which is shorthand for the proposition that "When others are doing it, you should too." In an appellate context on an issue of first impression, you might use this cue by showing what other jurisdictions have done when confronted with the same issue.

Another cue that is useful with heuristic mode thinkers is the *liking cue*. Have you or anyone you know ever been to a Tupperware(party? If so, then you know that it is virtually impossible for anyone who attends, not to buy something. Why? Because everyone who attends is presumably either family, a neighbor or a friend of the hostess and wants her party to succeed. In other words, the *liking cue* means: "When you like the source, do what is requested." If your court likes and respects you, subconsciously at least, they would prefer to see you win as opposed to a lawyer they find obnoxious and for whom the court has little professional respect. Do not get me wrong. Any such subconscious preference won't stop the systemic mode thinkers on the court from holding against you if they are convinced the law goes the other way. But, even if you lose, the language in the opinion may be soft enough to give you something to work with in a future case.

The final cue we will discuss is the *authority cue*. Back in the 1970's, one of the most popular shows on television was a medical drama about a family doctor called "Marcus Welby, M.D." in which an actor named Robert Young played the title role. Because of the show's popularity, a pharmaceutical company produced a television advertisement for a pain reliever that opened with Young wearing a white coat and a stethoscope, announcing, "I'm not a doctor but I play one on TV…" Despite the disclaimer that he was not a real doctor, his endorsement of the pain reliever caused sales to increase dramatically. The heuristic mode thinkers in the television audience bought the product because of the *authority cue:* "When the source is perceived as an authority, you can believe it." Find and provide precedential or persuasive authority for your position. If you do so, you provide an easy way out for the heuristic thinkers in your audience. What are other jurisdictions doing? Is there a law professor's treatise or law review article on the subject that shows a trend in the law you want the court to follow? The *authority cue* is also a shortcut for the impact of your reputation for credibility with the court and can make a difference in the outcome. When your audience is thinking, "If this appellate prosecutor says this is or ought to be the law, it must be so because he is always very well prepared and shoots straight with the court," you are considerably more than halfway home.

APPLICATION OF THESE PRINCIPLES TO THE APPELLATE PROCESS

Now that we have the basic building blocks of successful persuasion on the table, let's think about how to put these pieces together to win an appeal.

Start by keeping in mind four simple rules that will help your credibility (that *ethos* thing again) with both systemic and heuristic mode thinkers: (1) be prepared; (2) be accurate; (3) be clear and (4) be brief.

1. Heightened Standard Of Professionalism

You have to work with the record you have, and if the case was badly tried in the court below, you may have your work cut out for you. However, as an appellate prosecutor, you must also remember that you will be held to a higher professional standard by the court than your opponent. If there is clear error based on existing law, you will be expected to confess error unless you are arguing in good faith that the court should overrule the precedent that makes it error. Moreover, in a criminal case you will be held to the same heightened ethical standard as the trial prosecutor.

> Law enforcement officers have the obligation to convict the guilty and to make sure they do not convict the innocent. They must be dedicated to making the criminal trial a procedure for the ascertainment of the true facts surrounding the commission of the crime. To this extent, our so-called adversary system is not adversary at all; nor should it be.
>
> *Justice White, concurring and dissenting, United States v. Wade, 388 U.S. 218, 256 (1967).*

So how do you apply those persuasion fundamentals discussed above to the way you approach an appeal? For starters, you absolutely must thoroughly prepare your case and know and follow the rules of court. Failure to know the facts of your case and the applicable law will impact on your credibility in a very negative way. In addition, many appellate courts are sticklers for enforcing their rules, and the quickest way I know of to lose in an appellate court is to either procedurally default your position or effectively waive your ability to be heard. Failure to follow the rules of court will send your credibility into a downward spiral no matter what the thinking mode of your audience. Judges have long memories so ruining your credibility with the court also means that in addition to losing that particular case, you are now more likely to lose future cases as well.

2. Persuasion Techniques And Your Brief

> It is therefore ordered that the warden of the Fleet shall take said Richard Mylward... into his custody, and shall bring him into Westminster Hall on Saturday next... and there and then shall cut a hole in midst of the same engrossed replication... and put the said Myllward's head through the same hole, and so let the same replication hang about his shoulders with the written side outward; and then, the warden shall lead the same Mylward, so hanging, bare headed and bare faced, round Westminster Hall, whilst the courts are sitting, and shall shew him at the bar of every of the three courts within the Hall.
>
> *The penalty Lord Chancellor, Thomas Egerton (1603–1617), imposed on attorney Richard Mylward for submitting a replication (brief) containing 120 pages when, in the Chancellor's opinion, 16 would have sufficed.*

In an appellate court, you always get at least one opportunity to persuade your audience. That opportunity is your brief. Depending upon the court, you may also get a second opportunity in the form of oral argument. How might knowledge of the way your audience thinks and the rhetorical persuasion techniques discussed above be useful to you in winning the case on appeal?

Everything begins with your brief. An appellate judge must sift through hundreds and sometimes thousands of pages of briefs every week. Your target audience, therefore, wants to understand your case quickly and with as little reading as possible. To be brutally frank about one other related matter:

If your brief doesn't look good, you don't look good.

Your audience consists of people who read and write for a living; so understand that small things like spelling and grammatical mistakes can hurt your credibility. Seemingly insignificant mistakes suggest that you did not spend a lot of time on the case and have little invested in the outcome. Use the proper font size. Shrinking the font may help you stay within the page limit, but believe it or not, your audience will not go hunting for a magnifying glass to read your legal *tour de force.*

Do not just accept the issue as framed by your opponent. Frame the issues in your terms based upon your theory of the case expressed in a succinct but favorable way. If you are representing the appellant in a state's appeal, be judicious in the number of issues you present on appeal. Appellate courts do not give out an annual award for the "Greatest Number of Issues Presented in a Single Case." After two or three issues, the attention the issues presented will get and the credibility of the lawyer presenting them is inversely proportional.

Organize your brief well and use subsections to break down your arguments into more easily digestible pieces. Doing so will help you build your arguments in a coherent fashion, and it will also make it easier for the systemic mode thinkers in your audience to understand precisely where you are going and how you are going to get there. This is particularly helpful if you are arguing that you should prevail under alternate legal theories.

> It may seem ironic but most contentions of law are won or lost on the facts.
>
> *Justice Robert H. Jackson, formerly Solicitor General of the United States.*

There is no law that says that your brief must be dull and tedious to read. You can, and should, take the time to make it absorbing and understandable. Your statement of facts can tell an interesting and compelling story in a narrative fashion, provided your narrative is factually accurate and contains appropriate citations to the record. Try to make the judges want to rule for you. Tell the story relevant to the issues accurately and in a way that puts human values on your side.

For example, applying the principle of *pathos,* an excerpt from your statement of facts might read: "On May 7, 2003, the appellant, John Walker, abducted Sally Smith, a single mother of two young children, at knifepoint from the restaurant parking lot. She had just finished an eight-hour shift as a waitress during which she waited on Walker. Walker took Sally to a nearby wooded area where he cut the clothes from her body with his knife. He repeatedly raped and sodomized Sally at knifepoint and left her naked and crying in the woods. (T. 58–72) Sally positively identified Walker in a seven-man police lineup conducted the next day and in open court during both the preliminary hearing and trial of this case. (T.110–111 and T.83)"

Wouldn't you rather read that than: "Sally Smith testified that she is unmarried with two children ages 5 and 7 (T.58). She further testified that she was employed as a waitress at Joe's Crab Shack (T.59). Smith also testified that after finishing her shift on May 7, 2003, she was approached in the parking lot by a white male who she later identified as the appellant. Smith testified that the appellant displayed a knife and told her to walk to a nearby stand of trees (T62–65). Ms. Smith further testified that her assailant cut her clothes off and then held the knife in a threatening manner while he had sexual intercourse with her twice and oral sex once (T.70–72). Detective R.T. Jones testified that on May 8, 2004, Ms. Smith attended a police lineup that was conducted at the Detective Bureau and consisted of seven individuals including the defendant. (T.110). Ms. Smith identified number 4 as her assailant. Number 4 was the appellant. (T.111). Ms. Smith also identified the appellant in open court during the trial of this matter (T.83)."

Each of these statements of fact is accurate and complies with the rules of court in citing to the record, but the first is more interesting to read, is more likely to hold the reader's interest, and helps the reader empathize with the victim and thus your case.

After you have framed a concise, accurate and hopefully appealing statement of facts, a well-written analysis should follow. Your analysis of each issue should be cogent, easy to understand and supported by either precedent or logical extensions of existing precedent. In doing so, remember that an appellate judge is going to be more persuaded by the rationale for a particular rule of law than by bare precedents. In other words, show the court how to rule for you. Explain your legal theory of the issue and how precedent supports it, or why existing precedent should be modified or overruled. What your analysis should not contain is stream-of-consciousness assertions of case law, applied to the facts without regard for context or the development of the law.

Finally, take a lesson from poor attorney Mylward, what your brief is called is what it should be—*brief.* The most persuasive briefs are carefully crafted to do no more and no less than: (1) recite the background facts in a compelling way (but mindful of the standard of review); (2) apply existing statutory and case law to those facts in a logical manner; and (3) if necessary, explain how existing case law must be distinguished, extended or overruled to carry out the applicable public policy, legislative intent, or constitutional mandates. In other words, make your brief lean and mean and present your issues, facts and arguments with streamlined precision.

> The issues can be analyzed in pages less than fifty / if plaintiffs could with thought and words endeavor to be thrifty.
>
> *Asher Rubin, California Deputy Attorney General replying in rhyme to attorneys for the plaintiff's second request to file a brief exceeding the court's 50-page limit.*

3. Persuasion Techniques And Your Oral Argument

> I used to say that, as Solicitor General, I made three arguments in every case. First came the one that I planned as I thought—logical, coherent, complete. Second was the one actually presented—interrupted, incoherent, disjointed, disappointing. The third was the utterly devastating argument that I thought of after going to bed that night.
>
> *Justice Robert H. Jackson, formerly Solicitor General of the United States.*

First of all, my advice is that if you get an opportunity for oral argument, do not waive it. I am often asked if oral argument really makes any difference in the outcome of an appeal. In my experience it does—about 15% of the time. In other words, about 85% of the time, the way I vote to decide the case is the way I was leaning after reading the briefs and appendices. But 15% of the time, oral argument is the difference between winning and losing. In my view, that percentage is significant enough that you owe it to your client to give it your best shot if you have the chance.

Second, prepare for your argument. Re-read the briefs filed months earlier and update your research. If you find new cases on point, advise the court and opposing counsel in writing if possible before oral argument. This will enhance your credibility with the court and if the court finds a recent case on point that you missed, you will, or at least should, feel as bad as you will look. In the same vein, if you find a material mistake in the Statement of Facts and mistakes do happen to the best of us, disclose it immediately to the court and opposing counsel.

Third, your time for oral argument is short. Don't waste it on lengthy introductions or a restatement of the facts. Assume that the court has read your brief and is aware of the facts. Take advantage of the principle of primacy. Your first few minutes at the podium will be when your audience's attention is most focused on what you say so make that prime time count. Try to grab your audience with an "attention step," which is a 30 second or so summary of what you regard as the primary issue to be dealt with by the court. This attention step should state the main issue, convey your theme of the case, and set the stage for the argument in the way most favorable to you. For example:

> Good morning. I am Amy Decker representing the Commonwealth.
>
> The issue in this case is "does the Fourth Amendment permit a pat-down search based on the fact that appellant was standing in close proximity to, and conversing with, a person who is armed with a firearm."
>
> In other words, where one suspect is armed in an open-air drug market, is it reasonable for a police officer to suspect that his associates may be armed as well?

Next, let the court direct the argument. During oral argument, a judge will ask a question for basically only two reasons. The most common reason is that the court really wants your help in reasoning through the issue. You should provide that help by answering the question succinctly, honestly and forthrightly even if the answer hurts your theory of the case. Only then should you explain why the question as framed does not help with the analysis or why the question presumes facts that do not exist in your case or, if you must, why the answer that hurts you demonstrates why the existing precedent should be modified or overruled.

The other reason a judge may ask a question is not because the judge wants to know the answer; the judge thinks she already does. The judge asks the question so one or more of the judge's colleagues can hear your answer. The judge is using you to help her persuade the other judges. So if the court asks a question, answer it immediately and directly (again, do so no matter how much a straight answer hurts). If the judge asking this type of question is already on your side, the question will be a softball which you should recognize and answer in a way that helps that judge persuade her colleagues during the decision conference. If you don't know your case well enough to recognize a softball question when one comes at you, you may lose the judge who started off on your side.

Let go of those issues the court does not want to discuss. Typically, the judges will focus oral argument on the issue or issues that will be dispositive of the appeal. So, it simply does not matter that you see this case as turning on a single tenuous issue and that you have prepared to spend your precious time arguing it. If the judges are not asking you about that issue, the opinion won't likely focus on that point and, by the way, it probably is not a problem for you.

Finally, know when to sit down. If you sense that the court is with you based on the questioning of your opponent, you may not need to do much except to note that the court has already raised the points you wanted to make and offer to answer any questions. When you have nowhere to go but down, stop and avoid saying something that will result in snatching defeat from the jaws of victory.

CONCLUSION

If you understand and use these persuasion principles in planning, writing and arguing your appeals, you will not improve your chances of winning the lottery, you won't be more popular with members of the opposite sex, or drop twenty pounds overnight. But I guarantee that you will quickly develop a reputation for competence and integrity with the appellate courts of your jurisdiction, and you will be successful in those courts far more often than not.

> Appellate judges sit above the fray as the battle unfolds beneath. Then, when the dust settles and the smoke clears, they descend from their lofty perches and shoot the wounded.
>
> *An anonymous trial judge.*

ENDNOTES

[1] The "cues" discussed here are based on the work of Robert Cialdini. See R. Cialdini, *"Influence: Science and Practice,"* (2nd Ed.), Scott, Foresman & Company (1980).

TWO

WRITING THE BRIEF

J. FREDERIC VOROS, JR.
CHIEF, APPEALS DIVISION
UTAH ATTORNEY GENERAL'S OFFICE
SALT LAKE CITY, UTAH

Of writing well the source and fountainhead is wise thinking.

Horace (56 B.C.—8 B.C.)

An appellate brief should be brief. It should also be clear and accurate. These qualities are not the end; the end is of course to persuade the court. But they are the means, and they are a necessary means. They are the ABC's of briefing: be accurate, be brief, and be clear. No brief will persuade that violates these cardinal rules.

THE CARDINAL RULES OF BRIEF-WRITING

First Cardinal Rule: Be Accurate

An appellate brief must be scrupulously accurate. When a factual assertion is followed by a citation to a page in the record—and each one should be—that page, fairly read, must support the assertion. Likewise, when a case is cited in support of a legal assertion, the case, fairly read, must support the assertion. Statements of what a case means or holds must withstand a fair reading of the case. To cheat in citing to the record or to legal authority is both wrong and foolish: wrong because it is an attempt to deceive the court, foolish because any inaccuracy in the brief will be discovered either by opposing counsel or by a law clerk. Neither prospect is a happy one. If opposing counsel discovers the inaccuracy, she has an additional weapon to attack your argument and, inferentially, your credibility.

If a judge's law clerk discovers the inaccuracy, you may never know it, but the judge will. Most clerks begin life assuming that attorneys are thorough and conscientious, and are deeply impressed with evidence to the contrary. When they find it, they will feel they have found a pearl of great price that must be shared with their judge, or even included in a written opinion. You do not want your professional legacy to include this kind of reference: "In presenting this issue, defendant has not accurately represented the trial court's decision."[1]

Most crucial from the point of view of advocacy, an attorney who fails to be candid with the court will also fail to persuade the court. Of course, inaccuracy may result from sloppy as well as sharp practice. Unfortunately, from the judge's vantage point, the two are often indistinguishable.

Ensuring accurate citation is not difficult; all that is required is a thorough cite-check. The cite check should at minimum confirm or correct every record cite; confirm or correct every legal cite, including pin cites; and update all cited cases. Ideally, these tasks should be performed by someone other than the brief-writer; we all tend to miss our own lapses.

Second Cardinal Rule: Be Brief

A short brief is a favor to your reader. Judges are required to read a huge volume of written material. Part of this is our fault. Most briefs are written in haste, and, as a consequence, they are far longer than necessary. When we file a bloated brief, we cast upon the judges the burden of doing the final edit mentally as they read, and they like to edit our writing even less than we do. On the other hand, when we edit our briefs before filing them, judges appreciate it. Our editing makes their lives easier. Good editing is good advocacy.

There is truth in the German proverb, "Loquacity and lying are cousins." Generally, the more straight-forward the argument, the fewer words needed to make it. You need few words to say that the law and the facts are on your side. You need many to explain why a statute or case that seems to doom your argument really does not. Therefore, all else being equal, length and strength are inversely related. Judges know this, and it makes them suspicious of long briefs. For example, the California Supreme Court once stated that they were "inclined to doubt the correctness of the ruling of the court below, on account of the extreme length of the brief of the learned counsel for respondent in its support."[2] "Knowing the abilities of counsel," the court continued, "and their accurate knowledge of the law, a brief of 85 pages, coming from them in support of a single ruling of the court below, casts great doubt upon such ruling."[3] The court's pique was thinly veiled: "However, the learned counsel may not have had time to prepare a short brief, and for that reason have cast upon us the unnecessary labor of reading and extracting therefrom the points made. If we overlook any of them, counsel will readily understand the reason."[4]

Not only do shorter briefs look more persuasive, they are more persuasive. Usually, long briefs are long because they waste words. They digress or repeat or argue uncontested matters or make their point circuitously rather than linearly. They are difficult to follow, and their salient points are often lost in a clutter of words.

Therefore, after you finish writing, start cutting. Strike interesting but sidelight arguments. Strike empty fillers such as "Clearly," "The State asserts that" and "It is apparent that." In addition to adding needless bulk, these expressions convey tentativeness rather than confidence. Unless dates are critical, such as where defendant asserts a statute of limitations claim, include only one or two. Also, follow Mark Twain's advice: "When you catch an adjective, kill it." The same is true of adverbs. Nouns and verbs are strong; make them do the heavy lifting. Scrutinize long footnotes: irrelevancies lurk there. Shorten sentences and paragraphs. Tighten up.

Third Cardinal Rule: Be Clear

Clarity precedes persuasion. A judge who does not understand your argument cannot be persuaded by it. Oliver Wendell Holmes wrote, "I would not give a fig for the simplicity this side of complexity, but I would give my life for the simplicity on the other side of complexity." We are responsible for wringing simplicity from the complexity of the appellate record. The court is "not a depository into which the parties dump the burden of research and analysis."[5] We must sift through and present the relevant material in logical order. Your brief is sufficiently clear if an intelligent lay person can comprehend it in one reading. Keep it simple.

But how? For starters, put your main point up front. Do not bury it in the middle of a paragraph or in a parenthetical following a case citation. "Judges are not like pigs, hunting for truffles buried in briefs."[6] Do not hide the ball or unravel your argument gradually. You are not writing a suspense novel. A reader who knows your point up front can assimilate what follows, because he has a general framework into which to fit the detail. The opposite is not true: a reader faced with a mass of detail will understand none of it, because it lacks shape. Your readers should never have to wonder why you are telling them something. Transparency, not subtlety, is your goal.

To say that defense lawyers win by obfuscating would be an exaggeration, but it is not much of one to say that appellate prosecutors win by clarifying. In fact, if we cannot win by clarifying, we should not win.

THE PARTS AND PURPOSES OF THE BRIEF

An appellate brief has three major sections: (1) the Question Presented; (2) the Statement of Facts, and (3) the Argument. Each section should advocate, but each serves a different purpose. The purpose of the Question Presented is to frame the issue clearly, but in your terms. The purpose of the Statement of Facts is to make the judge want to rule for you. The purpose of the Argument is to show the judge how to rule for you.

QUESTION PRESENTED: FRAME THE ISSUE IN YOUR TERMS

Again, the object of your Question Presented is to frame the issue accurately, but in your terms. Like the rest of your brief, it should be accurate, brief, and clear. It is short, usually only a single sentence, but that sentence is the most important of your brief. The outcome of the appeal may depend on how the court sees the question before it. There is truth in the joke about the priest who was asked whether it was permissible to smoke while praying. "No," he responded, "that would be disrespectful." But when asked whether it was permissible to pray while smoking, he responded, "Of course. It is always appropriate to pray."

Crafting the Question Presented requires you to distill your case down to its essence. This is crucial work. Appellate law is a battle of perspectives; whoever persuades the court to see the issue from her point of view wins. Thus, it should be more than accurate, brief, and clear: it should tip the question your direction.

One way to do this is to include a key fact or two. In the following example, the defendant claimed a violation of his state constitutional right to appeal when the court clerk was unable to produce the court reporter's notes for the crucial day of trial. From the State's point of view, the central issue was not whether the loss of the trial record impaired defendant's right to appeal, but who should bear the risk of that loss. The defendant's issue statement was inelegant, but did emphasize his key point:

> Did the court err in not ordering a new trial based upon the inability of the parties to review the appellate record because the majority of the involved trial (i.e., court reporter notes of the second day of trial and trial exhibits) had been lost or destroyed?

The State's Question Presented included facts showing that defendant had caused the delay, which had in turn prejudiced the judicial process:

> Did defendant's absconding for seven years between verdict and sentencing, during which time defense counsel died,

the trial reporter's notes were lost, and the child victim grew up, so prejudice the judicial process that his appeal must be dismissed?

The court answered this question "yes." Here is another example. The defendant's Question Presented was commendably clear, but accomplished little more than identifying the topic of the appeal:

> Whether the trial court erred in denying defendant's motion to suppress on the grounds of entrapment.

The State's version includes three key facts that, if true, would defeat defendant's entrapment claim:

> As "the person who supplies marijuana for the town," was defendant entrapped when she approached confidential informants and asked them to front $100 for her drug run?

This statement of the issue illustrates how you can win a case almost before your start. If the facts recited in the Question Presented are accurate and not misleading, defendant was not entrapped.

Here is one more example of including key facts in the Question Presented. The defendant's issue statement, though brief, accomplished little more than telling the court that he was pressing a sufficiency challenge to a conviction for attempted sodomy on a child:

> Is the evidence sufficient to support a conviction of Attempted Sodomy on a Child, a Second Degree Felony?

In contrast, the State's version included every fact necessary to convict:

> Did defendant's act of exposing his penis and inviting a nine-year-old girl to perform oral sex constitute a substantial step toward committing the crime of sodomy on a child?

This issue statement is clear, brief, persuasive, and doesn't load the question. Once a judge reads it, the defendant will have difficulty winning.

By "loading the question," I mean the practice of tilting the issue statement one way or the other by including, not facts, but conclusions. Loading the question does not persuade the reader, but makes her think that either you do not know or do not care what the issue really is. Here is an example of a loaded question:

> Did the trial court properly deny defendant's motion for a new trial, where defendant's newly discovered evidence was discoverable before trial by reasonably diligent investigation?

This question is unpersuasive because it assumes what is at issue in the case, that the newly discovered evidence could have been discovered before trial. The following revision conveys that information, and, in addition, begins to persuade the court:

> Does evidence that defendant spoke with the victim's mother before the murder qualify as "newly discovered evidence" for purposes of a new trial motion?

This question does not merely claim that the evidence was discoverable pretrial, it demonstrates that it was by disclosing a key fact: the evidence was within the defendant's knowledge.

Most of the foregoing examples are questions ending with a question mark. The convention in some jurisdictions is to begin issue statements with the word "whether" and to end it with a period. They are sentence fragments, but custom and usage have over time forgiven the solecism. Some practitioners feel this form is too staid; others like it because removing the word "whether" leaves you with a usable point heading. Use the form your court prefers, if it has a preference; otherwise, use the form you prefer.

Time spent honing your issue statement, shortening and sharpening it, is time well spent. Write it and rewrite it, five times, ten times, fifteen times. Here are three versions of an issue statement that went through many more than three revisions. The case involved a post-conviction court that insisted on holding an evidentiary hearing even though the State had a winning procedural bar argument. This first version was accurate, brief (25 words) and clear, but not persuasive:

Can the district court properly refuse to rule on the respondent's dispositive arguments and order an evidentiary hearing on the merits of the petitioner's claims?

The second version was longer (32 words), not clearer, and not an improvement:

Is it proper for the district court to refuse to rule on the respondent's dispositive procedural arguments and compel the parties to proceed to an evidentiary hearing on the merits of petitioner's claims?

The final version was shorter (24 words), clearer, and more persuasive:

May a post-conviction court require an evidentiary hearing on the merits of claims that may be procedurally barred as a matter of law?

How brief should the issue statement be? Three lines, never more than four. Length and clarity vary inversely, but sometimes length is necessary to make an issue statement persuasive. If you must choose between clarity and persuasiveness, though, choose clarity, or you'll be left with neither. One enemy of clarity is clutter. Don't clutter up your issue statement with statutory or rule citations; just refer to the statute by name, such as the "Internet enticement statute" or the "criminal jurisdiction statute." If the statute lacks a name, give it one; it needed one anyway. You may be able to sneak in an occasional rule number if you are confident that your court will recognize the rule by its number, such as referring to the prior bad acts rule as Evidence Rule 404(b).

Should you refer to the trial court in your Question Presented? Your issue statement will be cleaner if you do not:

With reference to court:	Did the trial court correctly rule that a 22-inch zucchini is a "dangerous weapon"?
Without reference to court:	Is a 22-inch zucchini a "dangerous weapon"?

The disadvantage of this approach is that it omits the standard of review. If the standard of review is non-deferential, omitting it will not make your issue statement less persuasive. But if the standard of review is in your favor, including it will make your issue more accurate, clearer, and more persuasive, even if it is a bit longer:

> Did the trial court abuse its discretion in finding that a 22-inch zucchini is a "dangerous weapon"?

Some appellate lawyers prefer to phrase the standard of review in more positive terms on the theory that doing so casts the trial court in a more favorable light:

> Did the trial court properly exercise its discretion in finding that a 22-inch zucchini is a "dangerous weapon"?

I prefer the more standard formulation "abuse its discretion" on two grounds. First, it incorporates the words of the standard of review: it is the abuse-of-discretion standard, not the properly-exercise-discretion standard. And second, to the extent that any difference exists, I think the standard formulation, though negatively phrased, is more deferential. It sounds harsher, and thus more difficult to prove, to say that the trial court abused its discretion than to say that it did not properly exercise it.

In any event, your choice should be guided by the principles of accuracy, brevity, and clarity, with an eye toward persuasion. The purpose of the Question Presented is, after all, to frame the issue clearly but in your terms.

STATEMENT OF FACTS: MAKE THE JUDGES WANT TO RULE FOR YOU

Judges usually rule the way they want to, especially in close cases—not because they are biased, but because they are human. In cases at either end of the bell curve, the law points inarguably to one result or the other, and all but the most activist judges will apply that law. But most appellate cases fall more toward the debatable middle of the curve, where more than one result is legally justifiable, depending on how the judges read the law and the facts. In these cases, judges are to some degree free to rule as they want. So it is important that they want to rule for you.

This is the purpose of the Statement of Facts: to make the judges want to rule for you. By "want to rule for you" I mean that the judges' emotional sympathies and feelings of fair play make them hope they are able to rule for you. Legal argument is cold and left-brained. It may persuade your judges that they can or even should rule for you, but it generally lacks the power to persuade them that they want to rule for you. Only the facts can do that. Only the facts tell a story about human beings for whom the judges may feel sympathy, pity, skepticism, or revulsion. This is why "most contentions of law are won or lost on the facts," according to Justice Robert H. Jackson.

Before turning to how to make your Statement of Facts persuasive, let's spend a moment on how to make it accurate, brief, and clear. First, accuracy. In telling the facts of the case, you are absolutely bound by the record on appeal. If it is not in the record, it did not happen. And if it did not happen, it does not belong in your Statement of Facts. Every factual assertion in your Statement of Facts must be supportable in the record. The best practice is to include a citation to the record after every sentence. Accuracy also demands that you refrain from punching up the facts: if the witness said, "Tom got home around 10:30," don't write in your Statement of Facts that "Tom got home at 10:30." There's a difference; you see the difference or you would not have omitted the weasel word.

You are allowed to state the facts in the light most favorable to the jury's verdict. This means that in an appeal from a jury verdict, you can generally assume the truth of the prosecution's case and discount defendant's protestations of innocence. If a witness testified that he saw defendant shoot the victim, you can write, "Defendant shot the victim."

What about the circumstantial case? Can you, in your Statement of Facts, draw the inferences the way you know the jury did? The short answer is no. The better practice is to tell the facts as they were presented to the jury. At least one court believes it is "unprofessional conduct to represent inferences as facts."[7] You will have a chance to connect the dots in your argument, but your Statement of Facts should be just that: a statement of *facts,* not inferences.

What else should you *not* do in your fact statement? Argue. Refer to the law. Accept the defendant's Statement of Facts. Also, do not do a witness-by-witness recitation of testimony. That is a defense technique, designed to suck the life out of the story of the crime. Our culture is guided by the linear aspect of time: we are accustomed to hearing stories told from beginning to end. To tell the same story over and over from different points of view makes it difficult to digest. The reader must reassemble the pieces of the story in chronological order. The more of the burden of communication you cast on your reader, the less clear your message, and the less effective your communication.

Think of your Statement of Facts, not as a summary of the witnesses' testimony, but as a story. Do not summarize testimony; just tell what happened. So while this is acceptable:

> Dr. Hedley testified without contradiction that Sherman's death was caused by a sharp blow to the head from the wrecking ball.

This is better:

> The wrecking ball struck Sherman's head sharply, killing him.

Your Statement of Facts should tell a compelling story. A compelling story illustrates a theme that matters in human terms. It should catch and hold the interest of even non-lawyers. How do you tell a compelling story, especially when you are not allowed to punch up the facts? You cannot change the material, but you can select and arrange it. Select graphic details that put flesh on the story's bones. Especially useful are details that fix your story in the physical world or have an ironic edge. Also, ironic juxtaposition of facts will lend interest and tension to your story.

Your opening paragraph should hook your readers, making them eager—or at least willing—to keep reading. There are three ways to do this: (1) the flash-forward technique, (2) the opening summary, and (3) the straight chronology. The flash-forward technique requires you to begin, not at the chronological beginning of the story, but at its dramatic climax. Having hooked your readers' interest, you then fold back to the beginning and proceed in chronological order. The opening-summary technique summarizes the entire crime in a paragraph or two, then details the story in chronological order. The chronological approach tells the story in chronological order. It is the most natural and the easiest to write, but lends itself least readily to an opening hook.

Here is an example, with record citations removed for readability, of the flash-forward technique from a rape case:

> Defendant emerged from J.H.'s bathroom wearing rubber gloves and carrying a knife and a roll of duct tape. He put his hand over her mouth and threatened her with the knife. According to defendant, her frightened screaming aroused him sexually. He began to feel better when J.H., an adult woman, begged him not to rape her.
>
> Defendant had gained entrance to J.H.'s apartment only minutes earlier...

This fact statement opens at the story's climax. Chosen details paint a picture of evil, tantalizing the reader. Then, it folds easily back to the chronological beginning of the story. And, most important of all, it makes the judge reading it want to rule for the respondent.

Here is another example of the flash-forward technique and ironic juxtaposition. The issue on appeal was whether defendant was entitled to withdraw a ten-year-old guilty plea on the ground that he pled guilty to intentional murder, notwithstanding the shooting was unintentional.

> At about 10:30 p.m. on New Year's Day, defendant sat in a friend's apartment and filed a notch in the handle of his .357 revolver. He had killed Everett Hamby, Jr. about an hour and a half earlier...

First, if you are blessed with a case in which the defendant celebrates after murdering someone on New Year's Day, be grateful. Show your gratitude by exploiting that useful detail. Why is it useful? Because it allows you to include a strong ironic juxtaposition. The reference to New Year's Day, with its happy associations of confetti, noisemakers, and babies, sets defendant's death-dealing in sharp relief.

New Year's Day adds piquancy to the opening paragraph, but the crucial fact is that defendant notched the handle of the murder weapon. That fact alone refutes his claim on appeal: no one notches the handle of a gun with which they accidentally shot someone. In addition to drawing the judge into the story, this opening paragraph vividly advocates.

Opening with a summary of the crime can also be effective. Appellate prosecutor Kris C. Leonard crafted a powerful summary-style opening in a murder case:

> At closing time on February 15th, someone robbed the Payless Shoe Source Store in West Jordan, Utah. He took $849.73, a pair of size 10 men's "Attack" athletic shoes with teal trim, a pair of size 10(black "Honcho" boots with distinctive green stitching, and the life of the only employee in the store.
>
> However, he also left something behind when he left the store that night—an identifiable fingerprint on the employee's body.
>
> Margaret Ann Martinez was a 50-year-old mother of two at the time of her death. She had worked for Payless for nearly seven years…

Again, notice how effortlessly the Statement of Facts transitions from the summary to the chronological beginning of the story. But those opening sentences have changed everything: now, every pedestrian detail of Margaret Ann Martinez's life matters.

Those opening sentences have power because of the way Leonard has selected and arranged key facts. The second sentence is a list of four items. The first item is cash, stated to the penny. The second and third items are shoes described in puzzling detail. The final item is the life of a human being. Again, the ironic juxtaposition of the mundane with the sanctity of a human life magnifies the importance of the life, and by extension the killing.

Another source of the power of that sentence lies in the fact that the verb, "took," applies to the first three items literally, but the fourth item figuratively (the killer didn't actually take Margaret Ann Martinez's life away with him in his duffle bag). This is an obscure literary device known as a "zeugma." Leonard had no idea she was employing it, or that she was mimicking a passage from the final chapter of Harper Lee's *To Kill a Mockingbird*:

> Neighbors bring food with death, and flowers with sickness, and little things in between. Boo was our neighbor. He gave us two soap dolls, a broken watch and chain, a pair of good-luck pennies, and our lives.

After telling us what the killer "took," Leonard engages in a little word-play by telling us about something he "left"—his fingerprint. The killer left his fingerprint on his victim. This single fact speaks volumes to the reader: How difficult can this case be? Any errors are bound to be harmless.

Beginning at the chronological beginning of the story makes it harder to hook the reader, since the foundational facts are often mundane. But again, by selecting and arranging key facts, with an eye to ironic juxtaposition, you can build curiosity and interest in the story:

> On May 1, defendant purchased a red or maroon 1984 Oldsmobile. One week later, on May 8, he dropped in at a friend's shop in Brigham City.
>
> On May 8, Ashley H. was six years old and her sister Trisha was five. At about 6:30 p.m. that Saturday evening the girls got on their bikes to go to a school near their Corinne home. Ashley loved to be on her bike, riding the little course she set up at the school.
>
> The girls' mother, Deborah H., tried to walk down to the school to be with them, but the phone kept ringing. Deborah finally told the last caller that she had to leave and hung up on whoever it was.

Why, before picking up the thread of the story about Ashley and Trisha, does the brief-writer take such care to tell you about "a red or maroon 1984 Oldsmobile?" Is it just a graphic detail thrown in to add verisimilitude, or does it figure into the crime? Reading on, we find the girls gone to the school playground and their mother, who knows she should be there to watch and protect them, unable to disengage from friends calling her on the telephone, until finally she just "hung up on whoever it was." She didn't care. She was worried about her girls.

Just then, the mother testified, "I thought I heard my daughters' little prancing feet on the porch, but instead when I popped the door open to welcome them home, it was just [Trisha] dragging her sister's bike up on the porch." Trisha was angry.

She said that Ashley had fallen off her bike and then gone with a stranger. Trisha was very mad because she knew "that's not what we are supposed to do." Trisha said the stranger "took Ashley away in a red car."

There is the red car. We know who took Ashley. It was defendant. But consider two other details in this paragraph. The first is the language: "I thought I heard my daughters' little prancing feet on the porch…" Again, when the appellate gods bless you with a witness who utters poetry, your sacred duty as a lawyer is to include it. The second is that Ashley's abduction is told from Trisha's point of view. Trisha was mad because she knew they were not supposed to get into a stranger's car. In fact, Trisha has no idea of the enormity of the message she is telling. But her mother and the judges reading the story know well enough. This difference between the knowledge of the speaker and the knowledge of the reader has a name, "dramatic irony." It is a powerful literary device.

The foregoing examples were chosen to illustrate how to select and arrange material to make judges want to rule for you. Their records told dramatic stories. Not every record does. But every record contains interesting facts. Do not just regurgitate them. Sift through them for the well turned phrase, the dramatic moment, the ironic juxtaposition; carefully select your material and arrange it for maximum impact. Always be accurate, of course; be brief to the extent the material and the necessities of presenting it allow; and be clear. And do not forget to advocate.

Finally, what do you do with the defendant's version of events, the one the jury obviously and for good reason chose not to believe? I recommend putting it in the final paragraph or two, couched in words suggesting skepticism:

Defendant gave his version of these events at trial. He claimed…

Or:

> Defendant remembered these events differently. He claimed...

Perhaps here more than any other place in your brief, brevity is a virtue.

ARGUMENT: SHOW THE JUDGES HOW TO RULE FOR YOU

At last we reach the part of the brief that most practitioners assume does the persuading. But, as we have seen, every part of the brief should persuade. Having written the Question Presented and Statement of Facts, you have framed the issue in your terms and made the judges want to rule for you. But that is not enough. You must also show them how to rule for you. This is the function of the Argument portion of the brief. Every part of your argument should advocate, from the headings to the conclusion.

1. Use Assertive Headings

By the time you get to the Argument section of your brief, your main headings will already have been written. This is because your first point heading should be your first Question Presented, reformatted as a declarative sentence. Consider also using subheads within each point. Not only do these signposts make the text more accessible, they will also be gathered into your table of contents.

The table of contents is a road map to your brief. Upon picking up the brief, most judges will scan the table of contents to get an idea of what the issues are. Each of your point headings will become a main point in the table of contents, and each subhead will become a sub-point in the table of contents. So, you need to draft these with the idea that after you complete the brief, they will fit together into a coherent and persuasive table of contents.

Like everything else in the brief, your point headings and subheads should advocate; this means that they should make assertions, not just name topics. A topic heading does not advance your cause, or does so only by implication:

    A.   Preservation.

Such diffidence is unnecessary; assert your point:

    A.   This claim is unpreserved.

You might even want to explain your point a bit:

    A.   This claim is unpreserved because defendant failed to object at trial to the evidence he challenges on appeal.

Just do not abandon brevity. Two lines are ample for a subhead. If you use sub-subheads, a good technique in a complex brief, the same rules apply.

2. Follow An Obvious Structure

Like a well-written judicial opinion, your brief should proceed obviously and logically from general legal principles to a seemingly inevitable conclusion. After identifying appellant's claim, do not respond to the appellant's arguments point-by-point; affirmatively lay out the correct analysis. If your appellate court follows a customary pattern, consider using it as a model. Alternatively, the following sections lay out a clear and straightforward approach.

3. Identify Defendant's Claim

When you are appellee, begin by reciting appellant's claim in appellant's own words. Write, "Defendant claims that…" and then quote, from defendant's brief, his own statement of his claim of error. This may be difficult to find. Usually the defendant will at least state his claim in a point heading. If you quote a heading, remove capitalization, boldface, italics, and so on, and add a parenthetical to your citation explaining that you have done this: "Br. Aplt. at 21 (capitalization and boldface omitted)." If a single sentence cannot capture defendant's argument, add a second, beginning, "Specifically, defendant argues that…" and flesh out his claim.

Some practitioners believe that starting with appellant's claim gives it too much play. The first sentence of your argument occupies a position of power—why cede it to defendant? I see several reasons to do so. Even though as appellee you must reframe the issue in your terms, appellant is the one challenging the decision below. You must refute only the claim appellant makes, not the (sometimes stronger) claim he might have made. Therefore, defining appellant's challenge with precision, specifying what he claims and what he does not, is a crucial first step in your analysis. Before we start to argue, we must nail down what we are arguing about. Lazy, sloppy, or cunning appellant's counsel sometimes shrink from this. "Like a cuttlefish squirting out ink," in Orwell's phrase, they prefer to be vague about the nature and limits of their claim of error, perhaps in hopes that, as the appeal unfolds, a winning argument will emerge. Defining appellant's claim up front denies him this maneuverability. And defining appellant's claim in appellant's words protects against a later accusation that you have distorted his position.

Also, sometimes identifying what defendant does not assert is as important as identifying what appellant does assert: "Defendant's claim relies solely on the federal Due Process Clause; he makes no concomitant state constitutional claim...." Or, if defendant is challenging only one of a series of crime photographs, you might say, "Defendant challenges the admission of State's exhibit 14; she does not challenge the admission of State's exhibits 11, 12, 13, or 15." If exhibit 14 is functionally identical to exhibit 15, defendant's failure to challenge the latter may defeat her claim.

Finally, extracting a statement of appellant's claim from appellant's brief will help you avoid heading down a rabbit hole. Many an argument has required rewriting because an appellate prosecutor began responding to a claim without first defining it.

4. Summarize The Trial Court's Ruling

Next, summarize the ruling of the trial court. This is especially important if the trial court's findings bear on the issue before the appellate court or appellant failed to preserve the claim of error.

5. Argue Preservation

If appropriate, argue that defendant's claim is unpreserved. You might even want to emphasize defendant's failure by highlighting it in a lettered subhead. Do not stop at noting that the claim is unpreserved. Explain the procedural implications of that failure in your jurisdiction. In most jurisdictions, if appellant acknowledges the failure to preserve, she may still proceed under a deferential standard of review, such as plain error or manifest injustice. But what if appellant proceeds as if the claim were preserved? Will the appellate court still review the claim under the non-deferential standard of review, or is the claim barred altogether?

Whenever you argue that appellant has failed to preserve, you must consider whether to proceed to treat the merits of the claim. To rest on a preservation argument is perilous. You can do so only if your preservation argument is ironclad, your court is willing to ruthlessly enforce its preservation rules, and you can live with a reversal. Otherwise, the prudent course is to brief the merits. Conventional appellate wisdom holds that briefing the merits will give the appellate court the courage to enforce its preservation rules by demonstrating that doing so will not result in a miscarriage of justice.

6. Use The Standard Of Review

State the standard of review. Do not skip this step. Doing so is a rookie mistake; experienced appellate attorneys know that the standard of review is always important and sometimes decisive. And once you have stated it, apply it in your argument.

7. Set Out Controlling Law

Set out the controlling law. If the issue involves interpreting a statute or rule, begin by quoting the statute or rule verbatim. In fact, block-quote it, even if the passage is fewer than 50 words. When you set out the case law, begin with opinions from the highest relevant court, i.e., the United States Supreme Court on issues of federal law, the highest state court on issues of state law. Do not be beguiled by that foreign case with similar facts and flawless analysis; judges in your state care more about what courts in your state have said. They will not be reversed by the high court of another state.

8. Apply The Law To The Facts

Apply the law to the facts just as you learned in law school. Begin by laying out the proper analysis, much as you would expect to see it in the court's opinion. First show how your desired result is compelled by statutory and case law in your jurisdiction. Like the rest of your brief, your application of controlling law to the facts of your case should be accurate, brief and clear. Here are some suggestions for making it clear.

Apply the very words of the controlling test—not your paraphrase—to the facts of the case. Do not use variation to avoid monotony. It is better to monotonously repeat the words of the controlling test. If you use a synonym, the reader will wonder why. She said the officer had "good cause" to detain the defendant. Does that mean the officer did not have "reasonable suspicion"? The court has to apply the rules of the controlling test; you should too.

Proceed in logical fashion. For centuries, polemicists in the Western tradition have unfolded their arguments in syllogistic style. This is how the Western mind now works. Your argument will be clearer if you frame your argument as a syllogism:

Major premise:	A suspect's unprovoked flight from police in a high-crime area supports reasonable suspicion. *Illinois v. Wardlow*, 528 U.S. 119, 124–126 (2000).
Minor premise:	Defendant fled without provocation from police in a high-crime area.
Conclusion:	They therefore had reasonable suspicion to stop him.

Notice how inevitable the conclusion feels. This sense of inevitability is lost when the elements of the argument are presented in a different order:

Minor premise:	Defendant fled without provocation from police in a high-crime area.
Conclusion:	They therefore had reasonable suspicion to stop him.
Major premise:	*See Illinois v. Wardlow,* 528 U.S. 119, 124–126 (2000) (upholding detention based on suspect's unprovoked flight from police in a high-crime area).

There are two ways to bolster your argument with foreign precedents. The first is to demonstrate that the rule you advocate is the majority rule, or the trend, nationwide. Although string cites are generally disfavored, use one here, with a short explanatory parenthetical after each cited case. Read each case carefully to ensure that you are accurately representing its holding.

The second way to use foreign authority is to analogize to one or two persuasively reasoned opinions. Discuss the facts and reasoning of these cases in sufficient detail to persuade your court that the case is similar to the one at bar and that its reasoning is compelling. You may also combine the two approaches, beginning with a string cite demonstrating that you are in the majority, and then analyzing a representative case or two to show why the majority rule is rational.

After you have constructed your affirmative case—thereby showing the court how its opinion should look—turn your attention to defendant's authorities. You must distinguish any cited precedents from the United States Supreme Court and your own jurisdiction. You should distinguish any cited foreign precedents defendant treats at length. As noted above, foreign precedents are most persuasive in the aggregate. If defendant asserts that a majority of states or circuits favor him on a decisive point, you cannot let the assertion go unanswered.

Occasionally you will be faced with binding precedent that seems squarely against you. Rather than ignoring it and hoping it goes away, show the court how to deal with it. Appellate law is a battle of perspectives; you need to show that your theory of the case is broad enough to accommodate even an apparently contrary precedent. If your theory cannot accommodate it, you must argue to overrule it. If you have no basis to argue for overruling it, you must consider confessing error.

Respond to every defense contention, if only to say that a claim is unpreserved or inadequately briefed. If defendant throws in a reference to state due process, you must at minimum note that his nominal reference is insufficient: "Defendant also refers to the due process clause of the state constitution. *See* Br. Aplt. at 12. Such a nominal reference is insufficient to raise a state due process claim. *See* [case cite]."

Finally, in the appropriate case, make policy arguments, that is, argue that the rule you advocate would make the sounder precedent. Judges, especially those who sit on their jurisdiction's highest courts, do not have the luxury of adopting a rule for the pending case alone. Whatever rule they adopt will be applied by prosecutors, defense lawyers, and judges in perhaps hundreds of future cases.

This means that you must understand the implications of the rule you advocate. Of course, under your rule you win the case at bar. But how will that rule apply to the next, slightly different, case? To take one example, suppose the question in a case is whether a defendant's double jeopardy rights were violated. It is not enough to say that jeopardy had not attached here. You must have a sound theory of when jeopardy does attach.

Finally, conclude the discussion using the magic words of the governing test. Again, if you insist on using synonyms, a careful reader will wonder why.

9. Connect The Dots

If the State's case was circumstantial, your Statement of Facts should have stated the facts in the light most favorable to the jury's verdict, without articulating inferences. That doesn't mean that you never get to connect the dots; you just have to wait until the Argument portion of your brief. In a circumstantial case, the defendant is likely to mount a sufficiency challenge, claiming that the prosecution invited the jury to speculate from inconclusive evidence. You may respond by telling the story the jury reasonably inferred from the facts.

Here is an example from a State's brief. The victim, Lael Brown, was found shot dead in his own bed. His front door was locked and only he and his female assistant, the defendant, had keys to the house. (Record citations are removed for readability.)

> Without resort to speculation, the following scenario may be reasonably inferred from the evidence: Defendant needed money, more money than she had already borrowed from Clara and Lael Brown. With access to Lael Brown's checks, she forged checks to herself and negotiated them. Lael Brown received and reviewed the bank statement and, in keeping with his temperament, confronted her about the forgeries, perhaps threatening civil or criminal action. Defendant devised a plan to kill him to avoid potential felony charges.
>
> It was not difficult. She knew Lael Brown's habits and house, and in fact had the only spare key. After dancing and drinking with her boyfriend on Friday night, she arose early, drove to Lael's house, let herself in with the key, and retrieved the Colt Woodsman .22 from its customary spot, known to her from previous visits to the home.
>
> Gun in hand, she tiptoed into Lael Brown's bedroom and shot him in his sleep. Paulette Neiman and her dogs heard the shots. Defendant collected the relevant checks and bank statements, lifted Lael Brown's wallet, and left the way she came in—by the front door.
>
> Before 10:00 a.m., defendant disposed of the murder weapon and the checks, threw her clothes in the wash, and decided to take some soup to Lael Brown, a ploy to suggest both friendship and ignorance of his death. She left the soup on his porch, but did not go in. She returned the next day and witnessed her own handiwork. All that remained was to act the part of the distraught friend. Her only misstep was to claim that she saw Lael Brown sign checks that the State later proved were forgeries.

This retelling is based entirely on evidence presented at trial, but fills gaps between facts by drawing the inferences the jury evidently did. It makes explicit what must, in the Statement of Facts, remain implicit. Its power to persuade is palpable.

10. Minimize Footnotes, Block Quotes, And Outrage

Like everyone else, judges love to use footnotes, but hate to read them. One court, while conceding that "sparing use of terse footnotes can be useful," nevertheless complained that "the numerous footnotes in the briefs, some of which were quite extensive, served only to disrupt the flow of the text, repeat matters discussed in the text, or discuss matters that should have been included in the text or not at all."[8] Unfortunately, the burden is on lawyers to read what judges write, not on them to read what we write. This means that their liberal use of footnotes does not give us license to do the same. A good rule is to assume that your footnotes will be read by the judge's law clerk, but not the judge.[9]

Like footnotes, use block quotes with caution. Lawyers like block quotes because they make the job of writing an argument easier. You find a great passage in a case and just drop it in. The problem with block quotes is that they make the job of reading an argument harder. Also, readers tend to skip them.

Any quote over 50 words long must be set off in an indented block. If you want to quote a passage longer than 50 words, break the block into two or more sentences of fewer than 50 words each and include them in normal text. You can write, for example, "The court stated…" "The court continued…"

If you must use a block quote, introduce it with a complete sentence that summarizes the quote. That way, your reader will at least get the gist of the block quote, even if she does not read it. Do not fall back on the bad habit of introducing the block quote with a sentence ending in "as follows:" If you do, readers who skip the block quote will never know what they missed. Also, to draw your reader into a block quote, bold or italicize key words or phrases.

Block quotes are effective for one purpose: setting out a rule, statutory provision, or jury instruction to be discussed. Block quoting provisions you are comparing is especially useful, because the provisions stand out on the page, making it easy for the reader to see similarities and differences. For this purpose you may block quote a passage shorter than 50 words. In fact, this technique works best when the quotation is short.

Outrage and indignation have no place in any brief, but those of us representing the people must take particular care to avoid exclamation points, name-calling, hyperbole, sarcasm, personal attacks, rhetorical questions, and accusations. These are the written equivalents of screaming, pointing, and stamping your feet in oral argument.

Judge Gregory K. Orme of the Utah Court of Appeals chided one attorney for his "unrestrained and unnecessary use of the bold, underline, and 'all caps' functions of word processing" and "his repeated use of exclamation marks to emphasize points in his briefs."[10] "While I appreciate a zealous advocate as much as anyone," Judge Orme wrote, "such techniques, which really amount to a written form of shouting, are simply inappropriate in an appellate brief. It is counterproductive for counsel to litter his brief with burdensome material such as 'WRONG! WRONG ANALYSIS! WRONG RESULT! WRONG! WRONG! WRONG!'"[11]

From time to time opposing counsel will shamelessly misrepresent a case or the record. Resist the temptation to shout "WRONG!" Merely lay out the facts and let the judge experience the outrage. Juxtapose the misrepresentation, preferably a direct quote from defendant's brief, and the record or case quote, with a minimum of editorializing:

> Defendant's brief states that "the victim testified that she was attracted to defendant." Br. Aplt. at 27 (citing R. 382: 34). The record states that the victim testified, "No, I was never attracted to the defendant. His teeth looked like that guy in Fargo." R. 382: 34.

The unadorned facts will make your point more powerfully than "shouting."

CONCLUSION

The sum of the whole matter is this: write the brief you would want to read. When you write a brief, you are writing to persuade someone not so different from yourself. She has a robe, a title, and a lot more power, but she receives and processes information the same way you do. You don't like reading misleading, wordy, obscure briefs; you don't like having to puzzle out a brief's main point. You would prefer to read a brief that is accurate, brief, and clear; a brief that tells a compelling story, follows an obvious organizational pattern, persuades without deception, readily yields up its secrets, and does as much of the work as possible for you. That is the brief we should all endeavor to write.

ENDNOTES

[1] *State v. Pecht*, 2002 UT 41, & 48 P.3d 931.

[2] *King v. Gildersleeve*, 21 P. 961, 962 (Cal. 1889).

[3] *Id.*

[4] *Id.*

[5] *Williamson v. Opsahl*, 416 N.E.2d 783, 784 (Ill. App. Ct. 1981).

[6] *United States v. Dunkel*, 927 F.2d 955, 956 (7th Cir. 1991).

[7] *Skycom Corp. v. Telstar Corp.*, 813 F.2d 810, 819 (7th Cir. 1987).

[8] *Matter of Peter J. Schmitt Co., Inc.*, 154 B.R. 632 (Bankr. D.Del. 1993).

[9] *But see Washington v. Harris*, 650 F.2d 447, 450 n.2 (2d Cir. 1981) ("We do not accept the remarkable premise that the Appellate Division does not read the footnotes of briefs submitted to it."), *cert. denied* 455 U.S. 951 (1982).

[10] *B.A.M. Development v. Salt Lake County*, 2004 UT App 34, _ 71, n.30 (Orme, J., dissenting).

[11] *Id.*

> THE FOLLOWING IS A SAMPLE BRIEF TEMPLATE
> USED IN THE UTAH ATTORNEY GENERAL'S OFFICE.
> TECHNICAL REQUIREMENTS VARY
> FROM JURISDICTION TO JURISDICTION.

THREE

IN THE UTAH COURT OF APPEALS

STATE OF UTAH, :
    Plaintiff/Appellee,
:   Case No. ***-CA

vs.

:

***,

Defendant/Appellant.   :

BRIEF OF APPELLEE

AN APPEAL FROM CONVICTIONS FOR *** COUNT[S] OF ***, A *** DEGREE FELONY, AND *** COUNT[S] OF ***, A *** DEGREE FELONY, IN THE THIRD DISTRICT COURT, *** COUNTY, THE HONORABLE *** PRESIDING

                        ***
                        Assistant Attorney General
                        MARK L. SHURTLEFF (4666)
                        Utah Attorney General
                        Heber Wells Building
                        160 E. 300 S.
                        PO BOX 140854
                        Salt Lake City, UT 84114–0854

Defense counsel's name   ***
Defense counsel's address   Deputy *** County [or District] Attorney
Counsel for Appellant   Counsel for Appellee

[ORAL ARGUMENT and PUBLISHED OPINION NOT REQUESTED]

TABLE OF CONTENTS

Page

TABLE OF AUTHORITIES ii
JURISDICTION AND NATURE OF THE PROCEEDINGS 1
ISSUES PRESENTED ON APPEAL, PRESERVATION, AND STANDARDS OF REVIEW 1
CONSTITUTIONAL PROVISIONS, STATUTES AND RULES 2
STATEMENT OF THE CASE 3
STATEMENT OF THE FACTS 3
SUMMARY OF THE ARGUMENT ....
ARGUMENT
CONCLUSION ....
ADDENDA

    Addendum A—*Relevant statutes, rules, and constitutional provisions.*

    Addendum B, C, etc.—*Include parts of the record (such as jury instructions, written or oral findings of fact, memorandum decision, information, exhibits, testimony, closing argument) containing language crucial to the outcome of the case.*

IN THE UTAH COURT OF APPEALS

STATE OF UTAH,
:
    Plaintiff/Appellee,

:   Case No. ***-CA

vs.

:

***,
Defendant/Appellant.   :

BRIEF OF APPELLEE

Use Times New Roman 13-point type throughout the brief, including footnotes.

JURISDICTION AND NATURE OF THE PROCEEDINGS

This is an appeal from convictions for *** count[s] of ***, a *** degree felony, in violation of Utah Code Ann. (*** (1999), and *** count[s] of ***, a *** degree felony, in violation of Utah Code Ann. (*** (1999), in the Third District Court, the Honorable *** presiding.

This Court has jurisdiction pursuant to Utah Code Ann. (78–2a-3(2)(***) (1996).

ISSUES ON APPEAL, STANDARDS OF REVIEW, and PRESERVATION

1. **Issue.** *Some suggestions:*
   - *Do not accept the defendant's statement of the issue.*
   - *State the issue in three lines if possible, but not more than four.*
   - *Include key facts that advocate for your position, using the word 'where' as needed.*

Preservation. *State whether the claim was preserved. See rule 24(a)(5), Utah Rules of Appellate Procedure.*

Standard of Review. *Suggestions:*
   - *Cite one or at most two cases.*

- *If you are in the supreme court, cite supreme court cases if any exist.*
- *For sufficiency claims, cite Holgate.*
- *If there is only one issue on appeal, do not number it.*

2. **Issue.**

Preservation.

Standard of Review.

CONSTITUTIONAL PROVISIONS, STATUTES AND RULES

The following statutes, rules, or constitutional provisions whose interpretation is relevant to this appeal are attached at addendum A:

Single-spaced, full cites, including dates on statutory sections.

STATEMENT OF THE CASE

On ***, defendant was charged by [amended] information with *** counts of ***, a *** degree felony, in violation of Utah Code Ann. (76-***-*** (1999), and one count of ***, a *** degree felony, in violation of Utah Code Ann. (76-***-*** (1999). R. ***. *Cite to the statutes in effect on the date of the crime.*

Include further procedural steps, such as bindover, dismissal of charges, pleas to some charges, etc., as relevant to the issues on appeal. Omit dates unless they are relevant to an issue on appeal.

After a ***-day trial, the jury found defendant guilty [as charged] [of ***]. R. ***. Defendant was sentenced to the statutory terms. R. ***. Defendant timely appealed. R. ***. *To determine whether defendant timely appealed, compare the date stamped on the written judgment and sentence with the date stamped on the notice of appeal, in light of rule 4, Utah Rules of Appellate Procedure.*

STATEMENT OF THE FACTS[1]

Some suggestions:
- *Do not accept defendant's Statement of Facts.*
- *Do not argue.*

- *Tell a story; don't relate witnesses' testimony.*
- *Employ ironic juxtaposition.*
- *Start strong. One effective technique is to open with a compelling hook, then start the chronology.*
- *Follow every sentence with a record cite. Every word must be supportable from the record. Follow the wording of the record wherever possible.*
- *Do not include inferences, only facts testified to at trial—you can connect the dots in the argument portion of the brief. Of course, you can assume defendant's guilt.*
- *Make liberal use of short declarative sentences.*
- *Break up long passages with subheads.*
- *Include graphic, ironic, or well-stated details that give life to your story.*
- *If defendant testified, put his version in the final paragraph, using words suggesting skepticism.*
- *Unless dates are critical, such as where defendant asserts a statute of limitations claim, include only one or two dates (so when someone looks at the brief years later they can place the crime in time).*

SUMMARY OF THE ARGUMENT

Your summary of the argument should not exceed one page; in a long brief, two pages. Number the paragraphs to correspond to your argument points. Do not merely string together your point headings.

ARGUMENT

POINT I

[THIS IS YOUR FIRST ISSUE STATEMENT REFORMULATED AS A 3- TO 5-LINE ASSERTION, ALL CAPS, NO PERIOD]

Defendant contends... *Here summarize defendant's first argument in words quoted from his brief. You may have to search a bit to find where he has articulated his argument. Look at his point headings, then cite to them in this form:* Br. Aplt. at 4 (capitalization and boldface omitted). *You may want to add a second sentence beginning,* Specifically, defendant argues that... *and list his subpoints, again citing to his brief.*

A. The trial court properly...

This is just an example; you need not start with these words. But state your first subpoint in one to three lines. Use one left/right indent before the letter and one left indent after. Single-space, capitalize first word only, boldface, no underlining or italics, end with a period.

Proceedings below. *Here summarize defendant's motion or objection and the court's ruling, including any written or oral findings or conclusions.*

Standard of review. *If a standard of review other than correction of error applies, remind the court what it is with a cite to a recent case.*

Controlling law. *Here set out the controlling legal tests, in this order of priority: statutes or rules, Utah Supreme Court opinions, Utah Court of Appeals opinions. If the issue is one of federal constitutional law, include United States Supreme Court opinions (controlling) and Tenth Circuit opinions (highly persuasive).*

Analysis. *Remind the court of defendant's claim, e.g.,* Defendant contends that giving the instruction was error because "there was insufficient evidence to support the instruction." Br. Aplt. at 20.

Apply the legal test to the instant facts. Use the precise language of the test, not your own paraphrase.

At the end of your discussion, if appropriate, include persuasive policy arguments. For example: Moreover, adoption of the rule defendant advocates would... *then summarize the bad effects that might flow from adopting defendant's proposed position.*

In sum, defendant's contention that... lacks merit.

B. The trial court properly...

Repeat the pattern set out in point I.A.

POINT II
[SUCCINCT STATEMENT OF THE SUBSTANTIVE ISSUE]

Defendant contends...

A. This claim is unpreserved.

If trial counsel failed to object, say something like this:

"'[A] contemporaneous objection or some form of specific preservation of claims of error must be made a part of the trial court record before an appellate court will review such claims on appeal.'" *State v. Johnson,* 774 P.2d 1141, 1144 (Utah 1989) (quoting *State v. Tillman,* 750 P.2d 546, 551 (Utah 1987)). The objection must give the trial court notice of the "very error" complained of. *Tolman v. Winchester Hills Water Co.,* 912 P.2d 457, 460 (Utah App. 1996) (quoting *Beehive Medical Elec., Inc. v. Square D Co.,* 669 P.2d 859, 860 (Utah 1983)).

Defendant failed to preserve this claim in the trial court. *Tell what happened, with citations to record.*

Because defendant failed to preserve this issue for review, this Court should not address it.

If defendant failed to preserve the claim in the trial court and in addition fails to argue plain error on appeal, add something like this:

Furthermore, defendant does not on appeal allege plain error or exceptional circumstances. *See State v. Dunn,* 850 P.2d 1201, 1208–09 (Utah 1993) (setting forth elements of plain error); *State v. Irwin,* 924 P.2d 5, 7, 11 (Utah App. 1996) (noting that the "exceptional circumstances" exception is limited to cases involving "rare procedural anomalies").

This omission is fatal to his claim. Merely briefing an unpreserved issue on appeal is insufficient to satisfy the preservation requirement. Where an appellant "does not argue that 'exceptional circumstances' or 'plain error' justifies a review of the issue, [this Court will] decline to consider it on appeal." *State v. Pledger,* 896 P.2d 1226, 1229 n.5 (Utah 1995) (citation omitted). *Accord State v. Jennings,* 875 P.2d 566, 570 (Utah App. 1994) (declining to address issue where defendant briefed it on appeal, but did not assert either exceptional circumstances or plain error).

Because defendant failed to preserve this issue for review, and failed to argue either plain error or exceptional circumstances, this Court should not reach the merits of this claim. Nor may defendant raise this claim in his reply brief, since doing so would place the State in the difficult position "of either missing the opportunity to brief the... issue or having to construct and then rebut the unbriefed issue." *State v. Brown*, 853 P.2d 851, 854 n.1 (Utah 1992).

B. This claim lacks merit.

Repeat the pattern set out in point I.A.

If appropriate, add:

ORAL ARGUMENT AND PUBLISHED OPINION NOT REQUESTED

Oral argument would not significantly aid the Court in deciding this case. Because this case raises no novel question of law, a published opinion would make no useful addition to the body of Utah law.

CONCLUSION

Based on the foregoing, defendant's convictions should be affirmed.

RESPECTFULLY submitted on_____ July 20____.

MARK L. SHURTLEFF
Attorney General

***

Assistant Attorney General

CERTIFICATE OF SERVICE

I hereby certify that two copies of the foregoing Brief of Appellee were mailed this July 20____ to the following:

Defense counsel's name
Defense counsel's address

Counsel for Appellant

[1] Except as otherwise noted, this brief recites the facts in the light most favorable to the jury's verdict. *See State v. Litherland*, 2000 UT 76, & 2, 12 P.3d 92.

Other than this one, avoid footnotes if possible. Writers love them, but readers hate them. If you must use a footnote, do not place it mid-sentence, but at the end of a sentence or, better yet, at the end of a paragraph.

FOUR

SHORT DECLARATIVE SENTENCES:
The Key To Good Legal Writing

PAUL TURNER
PRESIDING JUSTICE
CALIFORNIA COURT OF APPEAL
SECOND APPELLATE DISTRICT
LOS ANGELES, CALIFORNIA

It has taken me years of struggle, hard work and research to learn to make one simple gesture, and I know enough about the art of writing to realize that it would take as many years of concentrated effort to write one simple beautiful sentence.

Isadoa Duncan (1878—1927), Dancer

The most important way to improve your legal writing is to develop the skill of writing the *short declarative sentence.* Some people do not need to use short declarative sentences. In 1995, the *Houston Chronicle* reported that Alan Greenspan, the Chair of the Federal Reserve Board, said, "I spend a substantial amount of my time endeavoring to fend off questions and worry terribly that I might end up being too clear." In 1992, the *Wall Street Journal* reported that one wag suggested that Alan Greenspan's tombstone should read, "I am guardedly optimistic about the next world but remain cognizant of the downside risk."

But as an appellate advocate, your job is to be clear; not to be uncertain like Mr. Greenspan. Your task is to develop the skill of writing the short declarative sentence so that words march promptly in proper order towards a logical conclusion. That statement of your mission warrants repeating. Your task is to develop the skill of writing the short declarative sentence so that words march promptly in proper order towards a logical conclusion.

Here is an example of this important way of communicating, and it is from the famous case of *Palsgraf v. Long Island Railroad Company* 248 N.Y.339, 340–341 (1928). It is the first paragraph of Chief Judge Benjamin Cardozo's famous opinion. In law school, professors use the *Palsgraf* opinion to discuss proximate cause and negligence. More importantly, it is the example of great legal writing utilizing the short declarative sentence as a way to communicate. Here, with minor bracketed interruptions, is the first paragraph of *Palsgraf*:

> Plaintiff was standing on a platform of defendant's railroad after buying a ticket to go to Rockaway Beach. [Stop reading now. How many words were the in the first sentence? 18. Now keep reading.] A train stopped at the station, bound for another place. Two men ran forward to catch it. [Stop reading again—how many words in this sentence that describes the hurried conduct of two different human beings in relation to a train leaving a station? Seven words—that is all; now start reading again.] One of the men reached the platform of the car without mishap, though the train was already moving. The other man, carrying a package, jumped aboard the car, but seemed unsteady as if about to fall. A guard on the car, who had held the door open, reached forward to help him in, and another guard on the platform pushed him from behind. In this act, the package was dislodged, and fell upon the rails. It was a package of small size, about fifteen inches long, and was covered by a newspaper. In fact it contained fireworks, but there was nothing in its appearance to give notice of its contents. The fireworks when they fell exploded. The shock of the explosion threw down some scales at the other end of the platform many

feet away. The scales struck the plaintiff, causing injuries for which she sues.

The longest sentence in this first paragraph of *Palsgraf* is 27 words, the one that begins, "A guard on the car…" That sentence consists of a series of short phrases strung together. Look at them: "A guard on the car, [5 words and a comma] who had held the door open, [6 words and a comma] reached forward to help him in, [another 6 words and a comma] and another guard on the platform pushed him from behind" [10 words and a period].

The most important thing about this whole passage is a reader knows exactly, yes, exactly what happened. This accident happened on August 24, 1924, at the East New York Station in Brooklyn and everybody who reads the first paragraph of *Palsgraf* knows what happened 80 years later. That is communication, that is the power of the written word.

Contrast the Court of Appeals decision with that of the intermediate appellate court. *Palsgraf v. Long Island Railroad Company* 225 N.Y.S. 412, 412–413 (1927). Look at the same rambling description of the facts in the Supreme Court Appellate Division case:

> The plaintiff was a passenger, intending to take a train of the defendant at the defendant's East New York passenger station, on the 24th day of August, 1924. [Stop and notice that the first sentence is awash in defendants. Also, that business about the "24th day of August," why didn't the author simply go ahead and say "the 24th day of August in the year of our Lord one thousand 900 and 24" and really make a long confusing sentence. Now continue reading.] While plaintiff was at the station waiting for her train, another train came into the station. After this train had started from the station, two young men came up and undertook to board it while the train was in motion. [Stop reading for a moment. Notice the two first sentences have two references each to trains. By the time the reader has finished reading the first three sentences it is unclear who boarded what train. Now keep on reading.] One of these men had a bundle under his arm. Two of the defendant's employees undertook to help him on the train while it was in motion, one of them the trainman and the other the man

on the platform. During their efforts to assist the man onto the moving train, these men knocked the bundle out from under the passenger's arm, and it fell under the train. The bundle contained explosive fireworks, which exploded and caused a large scale, near which the plaintiff was standing, to be thrown against the plaintiff, severely injuring her. There was no evidence to show that the passenger carrying the bundle had any authority or permit under the Code of Ordinances of the City of New York to carry or transport fireworks, or of the value of the fireworks, and it does not appear that the provisions of the Code of Ordinances of the City of New York (chapter 10, art. 6, § 92, subd. 6, Cosby's Code of Ordinances) were violated. [Look at the last sentence. It has 72 words in it. It is barely readable. It is poorly written.]

What is the point? There is a complexity to this factual and legal situation, whose train and in whose station the explosion occurs. Also, there are trains coming and going. There are people getting on the trains. There are people helping others get on the trains. A box is falling off a train as a person helps another person to get onto the train. There are a lot of things going on. But because it is complex, it requires that the sentences become even more simple and straightforward in order to effectively communicate. In other words, the more complex, the greater the need for simplicity and brevity. This is tough. Nobody can do this all the time. For some sentences or paragraphs, it just cannot be done. However, it is a most important step to effectively communicating.

Here is an example that transcends the centuries. It is translated from Hebrew into English but its style is consistent with the short declarative sentence style. Is this meaningful? You be the judge:

The Lord is my shepherd; I lack for nothing.
He makes me lie down in green pastures, He leads me to waters where I may rest;
He revives my spirit: for His namesakes, He guides me in the right paths.

That is the 23rd Psalm translated in the Revised English Version, and it personifies that short declarative sentence style. Note, it is more effective than any brief I ever read. Here is another example translated from Aramaic into Greek into English:

> Blessed are the poor in spirit: the kingdom of heaven is theirs; Blessed are the sorrowful; they shall find consolation; Blessed are the gentle; they shall have the earth for their possession.

This is from the Revised English Version translation of the Sermon on the Mount. Part of the impact of these words is that for many they are short declarative statements of faith and fact. But also, they are well written and this contributes to their effectiveness. Now it is unwise should try to insert the Ten Commandments or the Sermon on the Mount into your papers. It's bad enough when a plaintiff "prays" for relief in a complaint. Some of these prayers for relief are spelled plaintiff p-r-e-y-s for relief which may be more appropriate.

One final example of the short declarative sentence format. and it too lives:

> I was cruising in my Stingray late one night
> when an XKE pulled up on the right and rolled down the
> window of his shiny new Jag
> and challenged me then and there to a drag
> I said, "You're on, buddy, my mill's runnin' fine
> Let's come off the line, now, at Sunset and Vine
> I'll go you one better if you've got the nerve
> Let's race all the way to dead man's curve.

Now that, the first stanza of the Jan and Dean hit "Dead Man's Curve," is entirely different from Judge Cardozo's *Palsgraf* opinion or the 23rd Psalm. But the style is the same—short declarative sentences; albeit in a 50's rock genre. In all four examples, Judge Cardozo's *Palsgraf* opinion, the 23rd Psalm, the Sermon on the Mount and Jan and Dean's lyrical ode to a drag race, the words march promptly in proper order towards a logical conclusion. Contrast those examples to the verbose sentences in the intermediate appellate court opinion in *Palsgraf*. And contrast the enduring impact of the four examples of to the point writing with the completely forgotten intermediate court opinion.

Good writers strive to use short declarative sentences. Such writing is more persuasive than long drawn out sentences whose principal appeal is to the author. One note bears reemphasis. The greater the complexity of a legal issue—as a general rule, the shorter should be the sentences. Remember, Chief Judge Cardozo attacked a complex factual scenario with short sentences. The intermediate appellate court opinion contains long sentences. One opinion, that of Chief Judge Cardozo is remembered and admired; the other forgotten. You represent the people, your client deserves the best, and if Chief Judge Cardozo's writing is recognized as the best, write like him.

FIVE

WRITING THE PERSUASIVE BRIEF:
(And Some Matters Of Style)

TIMOTHY A. BAUGHMAN
CHIEF OF RESEARCH, TRAINING, AND APPEALS
WAYNE COUNTY APPELLATE PROSECUTOR'S OFFICE
DETROIT, MICHIGAN

Anyone can have the will to win. The difficult thing is having the will to prepare to win.[1]

Vince Lombardi

Only appellate prosecutors are in the business of doing justice. The job of defense counsel is to provide the best possible defense, and if that defense results in an injustice—the acquittal of a guilty person—defense counsel is not subject to criticism. The judge is a referee, insuring that the principal goal of the process—or at least that which should be the principal goal of the process—truth, is gone after fairly, according to the rules laid down. Defense counsel at trial cannot enter a guilty plea over the objection of the defendant, and defense counsel on appeal, faced with a clean record, cannot "confess lack of error," but at most only withdraw. But the appellate prosecutor may dismiss or reduce charges at trial, and may confess error on appeal, to effectuate the ends of justice. Where the ends of justice demand the affirmance of a conviction, or, in the case of an affirmative appeal by the appellate prosecutor from an adverse trial ruling, perhaps a suppression of evidence, or maybe the dismissal of the case entirely, or the seeking of review from a reversal by an intermediate appellate court, the appellate prosecutor on appeal is an advocate, and must act like one. The brief, from beginning to end, should be so structured and so written as to persuade disinterested judges of the correctness of the appellate prosecutor's position. This is not to suggest that shaded statements of facts, distortions of case holdings, or question-begging statements of issues are appropriate; indeed they are quite damaging. But it must be remembered that it is the judges that are disinterested, not the parties, and the appellate prosecutor must be an effective advocate for the People in order to fulfill the appellate advocate's duties. On appeal, this means persuasive briefing and persuasive oral argument. And no one can write persuasively without preparation.

PREPARATION

The bulk of an appellate prosecutor's time is spent in the role of appellee (respondent), filing a brief responding to one filed on behalf of a convicted defendant. Writing as the appellant is often more fun, for reversing a trial court can be more satisfying than affirming one, particularly when the victory overturns an order of suppression or dismissal while making new law in the process, or where it serves a needed educational purpose for the trial judge, while vindicating an aggrieved—and perhaps angry—trial appellate prosecutor. But sustaining convictions on appeal is the lifeblood of a prosecution appellate department, and consequently the suggestions here are directed, in the main, to preparation of the responding brief.

The appellate prosecutor should set the bar high, for as Judge Laurence Silberman of the District of Columbia Court of Appeals has said, "The best appellate lawyers will know about important milestones across the legal spectrum. They will keep up with new Supreme Court and… Circuit Court decisions… Appellate advocacy is, in essence, a business for legal intellectuals."[2] Simply keeping abreast of the ever-changing statutory and case law is required in order for the appellate prosecutor to be prepared to perform at that high level necessary to serve the public interest appropriately. Vigilance is required; the appellate department is no place for those who seek to escape or coast.

Give us the tools, and we will finish the job.

Winston Churchill

But diligence in study of the law is not enough for the appellate prosecutor; the appellate prosecutor must also write persuasively. Make no mistake about it, "[i]n law, the quality of writing matters. Good writing can win cases, and bad writing can lose them."[3] Few of us are gifted writers, and even those that are often need some assistance in insuring that their writing is sharp, concise, correct, and persuasive. The appellate prosecutor should have at the ready tools that provide this assistance. Strunk and White's *The Elements of Style,* Fowler's *A Dictionary of Modern English Usage,* Bryan Garner's *The Winning Brief* and *A Dictionary of Modern Legal Usage,* William Zinsser's *On Writing Well,* and similar works help provide the tools to "finish the job" well.

Betty Flowers, a University of Texas professor in the English Department, has devised a brilliant writing paradigm called "madman–architect–carpenter–judge."[4] The notion is that the writer first lets the "madman" loose to generate ideas, the architect then steps in to design the brief, the carpenter carries out the design, and the judge finishes the brief by serving the function of editor. Though this model is perhaps impossible to improve upon, for the legal brief-writer it may be added to. Before the turning loose of the madman—though the madman might fairly be said always to be active—what might be termed the "hunter-gatherer" must go forth. The appellate prosecutor should first read the appellant's brief to get a basic understanding of the issues raised, gauging their strengths and weaknesses, and making notes along the way. This should be done before the record is reviewed, as one cannot read the record with an eye toward the issues without knowing what they are. For example, on the face of the defendant's brief, a particular statement in closing argument may appear problematic, and so in reviewing the record the appellate prosecutor must be alert to anything said or done by defense counsel that would render the remark of the trial appellate prosecutor a fair response. From this hunt the appellate prosecutor will discern what to gather; that is, those cases that must be read or that area of the law that must be studied, the standards of review that are involved, and those portions of the record to which particular scrutiny must be given. Once the necessary materials, both factual and legal, have been digested, the appellate prosecutor is then prepared to call on the madman, architect, carpenter and judge to do their work.

WRITING THE BRIEF

1. The Statement Of Facts

In most jurisdictions, defendants convicted by trial have an appeal by right to an intermediate appellate court, or, in those jurisdictions without intermediate courts, automatic review of some sort in the state supreme court. Though appellate defense counsel faced with a clean record may move to withdraw, many do not. The result is that there are at least four kinds of briefs to which the appellate prosecutor must respond:

- *The downright frivolous brief.* This is what might be termed a "slow *Anders* brief," where counsel has chosen to brief something rather than withdraw.
- *The routine brief.* Though not frivolous, the case has no compelling facts, and presents no complex or particularly difficult issues.
- *The difficult or complex case.* Here the case may involve a lengthy and difficult record, raising multiple issues, at least some of which are complex.
- *The case of first impression.* Here the question is not so much the proper result on applying the appropriate law to the facts (and the discernment of the appropriate law that applies to the facts is in many cases the principal battle in the case), but what the rule of law actually is, where that question has yet to be answered, or, perhaps, the appellate prosecutor seeks to challenge the established wisdom on the point.

It is often said that the appellate prosecutor should always, always, always write a statement of facts, never accepting the statement of facts of the defendant. And, this sounds like good advice, if, as advocated here, the appellate prosecutor should seek to persuade from the beginning of the brief to the end. But for at least the first class of cases noted above, and often also the second, so long as the defendant's statement of facts is straightforward and reasonably inclusive, it may be accepted, perhaps with simply a few numbered additions and corrections. Appellate judges are busy people, and if a counterstatement of the facts can be foregone without damage to the persuasiveness of the brief the appellate prosecutor may accept, or accept with several exceptions, the defendant's statement of facts. Many prosecution appellate departments are like legal MASH units, where appellate prosecutors are generally overworked and faced with court-rule imposed deadlines. Spending time on elaborate statements of fact in frivolous or routine cases robs the appellate prosecutor of time needed for those cases where a statement of facts is important.

Where a restating of the facts is required, the appellate prosecutor must be sure to tell the story of the case. Because of witness availability problems, the trial frequently does not unfold in a manner that best tells what actually happened, or the truth of the case. The appellate prosecutor, while taking notes of the transcript witness by witness, must avoid converting those notes into a statement of facts in the same order as each witness testified at trial, in the manner of "witness Jones testified next, and testified that..." Not only is this method of summarizing the facts deadly dull, it is not persuasive, and an opportunity to win over the court with a powerful and scrupulously fair statement of facts is lost. Of great aid in the telling of the story is use of subheadings, not generally seen in statements of facts. These signposts for the reader can help engage the appellate judges, particularly when cleverly done.

Avoidance of overparticularization is also important to writing an interesting statement of facts. Facts that are unnecessary to the telling of the story—that can be omitted without compromising either its integrity or that of the writer in the mind of the court—should not be included. Unless critical to the case, dates are not often necessary, and the use of relative times helps the flow of the narrative. Why say "On April 22, 20__" when "Last spring" will do much better? Why use a particular date when a phrase such as "two weeks later," or "two months after he was shot," moves the narrative along more smartly?[5] The object of the writing is to be *read,* and the object of being read is to *persuade.* Appellate prosecutors must not lose sight of the goals.

Indeed, a powerful—and completely fair, as well as informative—statement of facts may be written without reference to specific testimony at all, though reference to pages in the record where the facts referenced may be found is, of course, necessary. One commonly sees facts written in this manner:

> Mary Jones was called to the stand. She testified that on September 30, 2003 she was waiting for a bus. While she was waiting at the bus stop a man approached her. She described him as obese, 5,' 7" or so, with a beard, and wearing a raincoat. She testified that he pointed a gun at her and demanded her money. He took $37 and some change. She testified that she later went to a lineup at the police station, where she identified the man who robbed her. She further testified that the defendant sitting at counsel table was that man.

More concise and more interesting is:

> On Labor Day last year, Mary Jones was robbed at gunpoint by defendant, whom she described to the police, and identified both at a lineup and in court.

2. Framing The Issues

Bryan Garner has said that "[t]here is no more important point in persuasive and analytical writings—and certainly no point more commonly bungled—than framing the issue."[16] It is impossible for the appellate prosecutor to begin to write the responsive brief without first fully understanding the issues in the case, for without this understanding the appellate prosecutor may unwittingly address an issue raised by the defense that is not actually presented in the case. More important than restating the facts is intelligently restating the issues presented. It is the rare occasion where the defendant's brief states the issues fairly, and it is quite common that an issue presented by the defendant is not, on close inspection, the actual issue at all. To meet the defendant on defendant's own terms is often to cede ground that could cost the appellate prosecutor a case that should be won.

For example, the defendant may claim that the trial prosecutor improperly used an admission in rebuttal that should have been presented in the case-in-chief. But in fact the trial prosecutor may have done nothing other than present extrinsic proof of a prior inconsistent statement of the defendant through the defendant's admission, after having laid the appropriate foundation, which is perfectly permissible. Or the defendant may argue that the search of a dwelling was achieved without warrant under circumstances where no warrant exception exists, when the outcome-determinative issue is whether the defendant had a reasonable expectation of privacy in the premises searched.

Issue statements may be divided usefully into four categories:

- *Signpost issues.* These do little other than tell the reader, in the most general terms, the nature of the issue.

    An appellate prosecutor quite commonly encounters these issues from the defendant. The defense statement of the issue might simply be: "The evidence was insufficient for conviction" (or, stated in the statement of questions or issues, "Was the evidence sufficient for conviction?"). While this might be a fair statement of the issue, it is at best a signpost ("an argument about sufficiency follows"), but does little or nothing to inform the court or advance the argument.

- *Question-begging issues.* These issue statements are not fair; they are in the nature of "when did you stop beating your wife," and undermine the credibility of the writer.

    At least equally as common as signpost issue statements are question-begging issue statements, where it is impossible to answer the question "yes" or "no." For example, the appellate prosecutor might encounter a question stated as "Whether reversible error occurred when the trial prosecutor improperly argued facts not of record in closing argument?" The appellate prosecutor cannot answer the question either "yes" or "no," for in fact the actual issue is assumed in the statement of the question—*did* the appellate prosecutor argue facts not of record, or instead simply argue fair inferences from the testimony? Accepting the issue framed in this manner makes it impossible to answer. And it is not effective. While appellate prosecutors must reframe question-begging issues, they must not counter with their own question-begging issue statements.

- *Persuasive issues.* These issues advance the argument. They are in that sense argumentative—but they are fairly stated, and do not beg the question.

Bryan Garner advocates a style of issue framing he calls the "deep-issue" method. While certain of Garner's ideas are controversial, such as his championing the placing of citations of cases—the "numbers," not the case names—in footnotes, the deep-issue method is far less so. Though there are those who criticize this method, when pressed they point to examples where the method is used poorly. Appellate prosecutors would do well to adopt this method, which eliminates the one-sentence statement of the issue beginning with the word "whether" or some other interrogative, but must do it well, and it takes some time and effort. The traditional one-sentence method generally barely scratches the surface of the issue presented, or is extremely cumbersome and awkward; in its place the issue should be written in the form of a syllogism, the conclusion of which compels the answer the appellate prosecutor is seeking. An issue framed as "Whether there was sufficient evidence for a rational jury to find guilt proven beyond a reasonable doubt?" is a useless formulation of the issue, telling the appellate judge nothing about the case, and failing to lead the judge toward the view the appellate prosecutor seeks to have accepted. It is a surface issue, and does not advance the appellate prosecutor's cause. But if the deep issue is whether there was sufficient evidence of constructive possession of the drugs to warrant a finding of guilt, then a statement of the issue may be constructed that informs the court of the rule of law involved, the salient facts of the case, and the conclusion that must necessarily follow, all in 75 word or less:

> Possession may be shown by evidence of dominion or control. The drugs were found on a nightstand in a bedroom occupied by the defendant. Could a rational factfinder find beyond a reasonable doubt that defendant had dominion or control over the drugs?

This statement of the question—which in an issue heading would be stated with the last sentence as a conclusion rather than a question—compels the answer the appellate prosecutor seeks. So long as the law is correctly stated and the facts accurately reported, the appellate prosecutor wins. And the appellate judges begin review of the case by so concluding from the statement of the issue itself. The deep issue syllogistic issue statement is concrete as well as persuasive. Appellate prosecutors should get in the habit of stating issues in this powerful fashion, but again, must take the time and care necessary to do it well. Further, if the statement is to advance the argument—to persuade—it must be read by the judges, meaning it must be 75 words or less. And it cannot beg the question. The issue stated above would be counterproductive if the second term was simply "Dominion and control of the drugs by the defendant was shown," with the conclusion then being that there was therefore sufficient evidence. On occasion the nature of the defense claim makes use of this method difficult. This generally occurs when there are multiple claims within one issue, as is often the case with both claims of ineffective assistance of trial defense counsel and "misconduct" by the prosecuting attorney, especially in closing argument. In these circumstances it is unavoidable that the middle term of the syllogism be somewhat general—though still not question begging—and particular points may be set off in the argument with subheadings.

Here are two other examples of deep-issue questions:

Example 1

Premeditation may be found where the defendant had the opportunity to subject his actions to a second look. The defendant retrieved a gun from another room and used it to kill the deceased. Did the jury rationally conclude that the defendant had the opportunity to subject his actions to a second look?

Example 2

Uncharged misconduct evidence is admissible if offered for some relevant purpose other than to show character, and the trial judge has discretion to exclude relevant evidence if the opponent of the evidence demonstrates that its probative value is substantially outweighed by the danger of unfair prejudice. The evidence that defendant murdered his first wife was relevant to intent by showing lack of accident. Did the trial judge abuse his discretion in admitting the evidence?

- *Analytical issues.* These are issue statements for the case of first impression, when the question before the court is to determine the rule of law, rather than to apply an established rule of law to the facts.

On occasion the case involves in issue of first impression, and so the issue statement is designed to impress upon the court what the rule of law should be, and, if discretionary review is being sought by the appellate prosecutor in the state supreme court, why the court should expend its resources on the case. For example, in a jurisdiction with no good-faith exception to the exclusionary rule, one might phrase the issue as:

> The exclusionary rule is a judicially created sanction for police misconduct that violates the constitution, and is designed to deter not to repair. The purpose of the exclusionary rule is not advanced when there is no misconduct by the police. Is exclusion of the truth in a criminal proceeding in the absence of some incontestable compensating gain an affront to justice inflicting gratuitous harm on the public, so that a good-faith exception should be recognized?

Or, a appellate prosecutor seeking to establish a rule that a knock-and-announce violation, when the search is otherwise proper under a valid warrant, should not require exclusion of the evidence discovered under the warrant, might phrase the issue as:

> Exclusion of evidence is only to occur when to fail to exclude would put the police in a better position than they would have been had the constitutional error never occurred. There is no element of causality between a knock and announce violation and the seizure of contraband pursuant to a valid search warrant and a search of proper scope. Does the Fourth Amendment

require the exclusion of evidence because of a violation of principles of announcement?

The statement of the issue or question is critical to the process. The appellate prosecutor can be fair and yet advance the cause, and can rarely do so by accepting the issue as stated by the defense.

3. Recognizing The Appropriate Standard Of Review

A claim of error cannot be addressed intelligently without recognition of the level of deference an appellate court is required to give to the ruling of the trial court. Is the standard of review abuse of discretion, clear error, de novo review by the appellate court, or some combination of these standards? If the issue is forfeited by a failure to make a contemporaneous objection, review is for plain error, a standard that is extremely difficult for the defense to meet, and quite often ignored in the defendant's brief, which treats the issue as though it were preserved. The appellate prosecutor must discern the appropriate standard of review, build the argument around it, and even work it into the statement of the issue (for example, "Evidence is relevant if it has any tendency in logic to make a fact of consequence more or less probable than it would be without the evidence. The trial judge found that the autopsy photographs showing a contact wound were relevant to negate the claim of self-defense. The trial judge did not abuse his discretion in admitting the autopsy photographs").

4. Organizing The Response

As with the statement of facts, substantive subheadings that make a positive statement advancing the argument, and provide signposts for the appellate judge, are extremely useful. Fashioning them is a part of the work required by the architect before the writing begins. Also, too often the appellate prosecutor writes defensively, parroting the claim of the defendant and then attempting to defeat it. It is far more persuasive to make the appellate prosecutor's case by proving the deep-issue statement that heads the particular argument in an affirmative manner. This does not mean counterarguments should not be addressed. But the appellate prosecutor should proceed in dialectical form: assert the legal premise, discuss the facts relevant to the question, and draw the conclusion, and only then proceed to the counterarguments. Having reached the appropriate conclusion, the appellate prosecutor may point out that "it may be argued, on the other hand, that…" but "this argument fails because…" And "it might further be advanced that" but "this argument is also unavailing for the reason that…"[7]

5. Handling Authority

If the object of having the brief read, so as to accomplish the goal of persuading the appellate judges, is to be met, then the appellate prosecutor must avoid string citations and lengthy block quotations. If there is a controlling case it is wise to cite it and move on. If there are helpful illustrative cases, these should be discussed in more detail in the text, or placed in a footnote with a parenthetical sentence noting the point of similarity. Also, appellate judges are busy, and they find block quotes unhelpful. They simply will not read them. If quoting rather than paraphrasing is deemed advisable, then quote no more than necessary. If a large block quote contains all the necessary factors of a multi-prong legal test, then break the quote into component parts and use bullets to create a list. The judges will read the bulleted list where they will not read a large block quote.

Judges also detest substantive footnotes. Except on rare occasions footnotes should be reserved for citations, and substantive material should be included in the text. If the footnote is truly an aside, consider whether it should be eliminated completely. Though many judges would disagree, there is a reasonable argument for a place for substantive footnotes in the complex case, particularly the case of first impression. Often historical materials that may set an issue in context, but which some of the judges or justices may find helpful to the argument and some may not, can be put in footnotes. Knowing the court and the judges on the court is necessary to deciding whether to include some substantive footnotes of this sort.

It is not only unwise but unethical to avoid citing and confronting contrary authority. If a case appears to harm the prosecution position but is distinguishable, distinguish it. If it is not distinguishable but arguably wrongly decided confront it head on and argue it is wrong. Perhaps the legal principle involved is one that needs further review from the state's highest court.

6. Editing The Brief: The Work Of The "Judge"

Though the architect should carefully design the structure of the argument before the carpenter begins the work of writing, the carpenter must write without interference from the judge. Editing comes after the writing, not during it. Write an issue straight through, set it aside, and then return to it later for editing. Many find it hard to edit on a computer screen, and instead print out the draft, taking their own red pen to it. The tools mentioned previously are important aids to the editing process. The writing should be grammatically correct, concise and polished. The writer should be ruthless in editing, and the brief should be read also by someone other than the writer. This is important not only so as to gain the perspective of someone removed from the writing itself, but also because it is very easy to read over errors.

STYLE AND MECHANICS

Clarity is critical in order to persuade, and the appellate prosecutor's brief should be uncluttered and direct. Particularly when the office has an appellate department, principles should be established that insure that there is consistency in the work product, including its appearance. Among the points to bear in mind are:

Type size and font. The formatting must comply with applicable court rules, and should be consistent from brief to brief, and attorney to attorney in an appellate department.

Emphasis. Do not overuse typographic methods of emphasis, as the writing should speak for itself. When typographic emphasis is employed, consider using italics rather than underlining or boldface.

Block Quotations. Do not use quotation marks to set off block quotations. For quotations within a block quotation use ordinary quotation marks, not single marks. A citation identifying the source of the block quotation, if appearing after the block quotation, should be double spaced from the quotation and lined up with the left side of the quotation. Text should then continue double spaced from the citation, either flush with the left margin if the paragraph continues, or indented if a new paragraph is started. Lengthy block quotations should be avoided. If the writer believes that the quotation cannot effectively be paraphrased, one way to avoid the long block of type is to break up the quotation by using bullet points with the text in each point single spaced, but the points set off by a double space, even though the entire quotation is presented without paraphrase.

Passive Voice. Be particularly careful here to avoid the passive voice, which lessens the force of argument (for example, use "The defendant murdered the victim" rather than "the victim was murdered").

Avoid Clutter. Avoid overuse of "clearly," "obviously," "plainly" and the like. Remove "throat clearing" phrases, such as "The People would submit that" or "It is important to note that."

Such/Pronoun. Do not use "such" as a pronoun or article.

Strong Verbs And Nouns. Use strong verbs and nouns and avoid overuse of adjectives. As Mark Twain said, "when you catch adjectives, kill most of them—then the rest will be valuable. They weaken when they are close together; they give strength when they are wide apart."

Legalese. In addition to avoiding clutter, avoid legalese. And, do not use "prior to" when "before" can be used, or "subsequent to" when what is meant is "after" or "later." Instead of "Prior to trial the defendant moved to suppress" say, "Before trial the defendant moved to suppress."

CONCLUSION

An appellate prosecutor's most valuable asset is his or her reputation, and this is as true for appellate prosecutors as trial appellate prosecutors. To paraphrase Mark Twain, the appellate prosecutor as advocate must always do right, for this will gratify most people, and astonish the rest. There is no room for sharp practice in a appellate prosecutor's appellate brief. The facts must be told in an interesting manner and engaging manner, but the statement of facts must be accurate, and unhelpful facts included. The argument must be persuasive and hold the attention of the judges, but a contrary case cannot be avoided, the meaning of a case cannot be shaded, and the argument cannot be strained. Further, there is no place for hyperbole or personal attacks on opposing counsel or the lower court.

But this does not mean the appellate prosecutor is not an advocate. The appellate prosecutor has a client, the People of the State, and owes to them a duty of zealous advocacy. To fulfill this duty owed the People, and to continue to deserve the privilege of representing them, the appellate prosecutor must write powerfully and persuasively, with a thorough understanding of the issues and the law. An appellate prosecutor who gains a reputation with the appellate courts as an "interesting read," and a trustworthy and sound advocate, has a distinct advantage, and serves the public well and honorably.

ENDNOTES

[1] Attributed to Vince Lombardi or Bobby Knight, depending on the source used.

[2] Hon. Laurence Silberman, Judge of the United States Court of Appeals for the District of Columbia Circuit, ABA Journal, *Litigation*, Spring, 1994.

[3] Bryan A. Garner, *The Winning Brief*, (Oxford University Press: 1999), p.ix.

[4] Betty S. Flowers, "Madman, Architect, Carpenter, Judge: Roles and the Writing Process," 44 Proceedings of the Conference of College Teachers of English, p. 7-10 (1979).

[5] See Hon. Thomas Gee, "A Few of Wisdom's Idiosyncrasies and a Few of Ignorance's: A Judicial Style Sheet," 1 Scribes J. Legal Writing 55, 56 (1990).

[6] Bryan A. Garner, *A Dictionary of Modern Legal Usage* (Oxford University Press: 1995), p. 471.

[7] See Garner, *The Winning Brief*, Tip 88.

SIX

APPELLATE STRATEGIES

ROBERT M. FOSTER
SUPERVISING DEPUTY ATTORNEY GENERAL
CALIFORNIA ATTORNEY GENERAL'S OFFICE
SAN DIEGO, CALIFORNIA

There is always a best way to do everything. If it be to boil an egg.

Ralph Waldo Emerson (1803—1882)

An appellate prosecutor must be aware of the tactical and strategic issues involved in any post-conviction criminal appeal. There are considerations involved in every such case that transcend any legal or factual issues within the case. These factors often play a role in the ability of the appellate prosecutor to accomplish the primary appellate goal: to persuade the appellate court to affirm the just conviction and sentence imposed in the trial court. This is more than a mere mechanical undertaking. This chapter discusses appellate strategies for accomplishing this major goal.

CREDIBILITY ENHANCEMENT AND PITFALLS

A raft of secondary goals arises in every appeal. It is of little value to win an appeal, if, in doing so, the secondary goals are lost. Perhaps of primary importance is credibility. There are two aspects to this issue: the general credibility of your office and the personal credibility of the particular appellate prosecutor. If credibility is lost, it will undercut the primary goal of persuasiveness in the case at hand and in future cases before the appellate court.

The credibility of an office is usually established long before an appellate prosecutor begins work on a particular case. But, it is important to realize that each court probably has a pre-existing evaluation of the offices that regularly appear in front of the court. The higher that reputation is, the more important it is for each appellate prosecutor to strive to ensure that the advocate's work meets or exceeds that standard. On cutting edge issues, the office should present a united front to the court. An office that presents conflicting arguments to an appellate court in different cases but on the same point of law will appear disorganized and careless. Care must be taken to assure that one position in one case does not end up undercutting the office's position in several other cases.

Personal credibility is more elusive. But, remember that a reputation carefully honed over the years can rapidly be diminished by a major mistake in a single case. An appellate justice once commented that there are two critical factors that an appellate advocate must understand about appellate justices: they have memories like elephants and they love to gossip. What does this mean for the appellate prosecutor? It means that in every case your personal credibility is at issue. In a situation where the court concludes you have egregiously violated some basic rule, or that you have intentionally misled the court, they will remember it and will probably share that conclusion with their brethren. Your personal credibility will suffer. No case, no result is worth the sacrifice of your personal credibility with the court.

Five areas most often seem to damage the appellate prosecutor's personal credibility. The first pitfall is inexcusable inaccuracy. It is critical that every citation to the record be totally accurate. You represent the prosecution, and if the court cannot rely on you for accuracy, you have lost most of your persuasive force. While a respondent has the right to present the record in the light most favorable to the decision of the trier of fact, care must be taken to ensure that every assertion of fact has a basis in the record. In situations where an advocate is uncertain, a footnote explaining the situation will ensure the court's understanding. As an example: "The record does not indicate where in the defendant's car the police found the murder weapon." In other situations, use of the word "apparently" may alert the court to the issue: "Apparently the witness told the officer she had heard nothing because the officer left her apartment and walked around the building looking for signs of entry." But, your reputation depends on you accurately citing to the record.

The second problem is use of unsupported hyperbole. The use of such an overreaching literary device is normally self destructive. Describing a bank robber as the worst fiend since Jessie James is unpersuasive and thus self defeating. Often a respondent is tempted to make an argument concerning what the consequences will be if a particular appellant's argument is accepted. Care must be taken so that the consequences will not be overstated. Suggesting the crumbling of modern day society if the court follows an appellant's argument is unpersuasive and should be avoided.

Third, the respondent's brief should not contain unwarranted screaming. Most appellate justices prefer briefs carefully drafted to effectively persuade without resort to heavy-handed overstatements. A moderate tone, urging the court to adopt the respondent's position is far more effective than a brief that goes to linguistic summits again and again. While one such zenith may be effective in a brief, the repeated use becomes irritating. Often, when the author tries to show the appellate court how glib she can be, or how many modern song titles or cultural icons can be worked into the brief, all the writer does is convey a sense of intellectual arrogance that alienates the reader. The goal, of course, is to sway the appellate justices, not alienate them. In this vein, any and all references to *Alice in Wonderland,* the most over quoted work of fiction in legal writing, should be avoided at all costs.

Fourth, the use of personalities and insults directed toward opposing counsel are absolutely improper. It will simply damage the appellate prosecutor's credibility. While most appellate justices enjoy a contested intellectual battle over an idea, they detest any personal combat between the litigants using flaming epithets. The appellate justices' cases are filled with violence, and normally they are most assertive in their drive to ensure such events remain well outside their courtrooms and chambers.

Appellate courts normally take great exception to personal attacks and have been known to strike documents or conduct contempt hearings for attorneys who violate this rule. One Petition for Certiorari at the

Supreme Court of the United States contained a paragraph in which Petitioner's counsel tore into the ethics of the United States Attorney involved in the case. The petition stated, "... It is outrageous that an office of the United States and supposedly advised of the rudiments of ethical conduct should advance frivolous arguments merely for the purpose of delay and should dare to use so contemptible and obviously dilatory a device which outrages common decency." The court struck the brief. While it may have been that the Petition had a valid legal point, the issue was so badly framed, so filed with personal invective, that it lost all persuasive force. Calm understatement is not lost on most appellate courts.

Care must be taken to differentiate between an attack on an idea and an attack on the proponent of the idea. It is one thing to say that a particular claim is misleading because it emphasizes the wrong issues. Such an assertion would be proper. It is a far different thing to say that counsel is trying to mislead the court with the argument. While a fine line exists between it is a critical difference that must be recognized. The first example deals with an idea; the second with counsel's character.

Finally, the use of inappropriate humor can totally alienate an appellate court. Attempts at humor that so often depend on the tone or inflection of the speaker when delivered in written form can easily come across as snide or condescending. Attempts at humor are best left unwritten and unsaid. Even though you may be appearing before an appellate justice known for humorous opinions, leave the levity to the court. You run the risk of losing credibility by a wry aside that falls flat or insults the intelligence.

KNOW YOUR COURT

It is impossible to emphasize this point too heavily—know your court. Every appellate court has a unique personality. The obvious main distinction is the orientation of the court. As has been seen in recent years there is a wide difference between the Ninth Circuit and the Supreme Court of the United States. An appellate advocate must take the time to learn the nature and character of the court. Aside from a liberal or conservative bent, many courts have particular issues that raise their ire. For instance, one court may have a particular problem with cases involving the improper exclusion of jurors for reasons that are not race neutral. Another court may have a problem with cases involving the good faith exception to the hearsay rule. An effective advocate needs to know the court's orientation.

An effective appellate prosecutor must be aware of any particular idiosyncrasies of the court. Writing a detailed Brandeis style brief for a court that has a strong preference for short, nuts and bolts kinds of discussion and analysis may be a crowning achievement in research and drafting but a miserable failure because it was written for a different audience.

Learning a particular court's outlook and approach is often no easy task. But, certain steps can help an advocate gain insight. The first step, of course, is to read the written opinions from the court. Reading every opinion that issues from the court, in both criminal and civil cases, can often provide valuable insights into critical issues. Even if some of the opinions of the court are unpublished, the clerk's office normally has a file where such documents can be read. Some of the electronic legal research services now present such unpublished materials. An opinion may also yield particular phrases repeatedly used by the court and therefore use of them in the brief and argument may add to the persuasive force. One California appellate court was particularly fond of the phrase: "Not so." After observing this proclivity on the part of the court, the respondent's briefs began using the phrase as an introductory response to an appellant's erroneous claim of error.

Another source of information is attorneys who have appeared in front of the court for years. More experience colleagues either in your own office or in other governmental agencies can provide a wealth of information. It may yield insights into the character or personality of each of the justices. An advocate may learn that one justice likes to use oral argument as an intellectual exercise and to see how swift an advocate can be on her feet. Think of a cat playfully toying with a ball of yarn. An advocate may learn that another justice seldom speaks but when he does, the justice always manages to disclose his position on a case. Other justices may have a delivery that makes them sound angry or upset when they are merely inquisitive.

Often law libraries publish legal biographies that may give detailed background information including prior employment history, hobbies and written articles that may give further insights into a justice.

Major sources of information, far too often untapped, are the court clerks. Often a call to the court clerk asking what the court likes and dislikes will elicit large amounts of information. Far too often the court clerks simply receive calls from secretaries or lawyers assistants requesting information for the appellate advocate. A lawyer who takes the time to chat with the clerk will often be rewarded with assistance or suggestions that might not otherwise be forthcoming. Indeed, across a career many such long-term contacts can be achieved and used repeatedly to the benefit of both the advocate and the clerk. Of course, such discussions should never go to the merits, but they may be able to resolve questions such as the format the court prefers for a certain type of response. In other instances, the clerk may be able to help resolve problems with the service or filing of a document or to provide an explanation of how the court views a particular rule concerning the filing of a document.

If at all possible, watch the court during oral argument on a day prior to your own argument can be invaluable. This is especially true for cases at the Supreme Court of the United States. The courtroom itself, with its Sienna marble columns, Spanish marble walls and mahogany bench, is impressive almost beyond words. The history of that room, the cases that have been argued there, are awe inspiring. Moreover, seeing all nine of the justices suddenly emerge from behind the dark red curtain precisely at 10:00 a.m. can be breathtaking. Seeing, in person, the faces you have seen regularly on the news, is impressive. Given these factors, an appellate advocate must spend some time just sitting and watching the Supreme Court's oral arguments. Spending a day just watching can assuage many of the fears and give counsel a sense of what is to come. The same is often true for any other appellate courtroom.

Here again is a situation where the court's clerks can be extremely helpful. A brief conversation with most of the Clerks at the Supreme Court of the United States will yield the fact that the Supreme Court does not like the use of charts, maps or diagrams in most oral arguments. Having witnessed an oral argument in which an advocate tried to repeatedly use a Bible and an apple to make his point and only succeeded in irritating several members of the court, it was obvious that he had not talked to the clerks about such theatrical props. The argument suffered as a result. He lost 9–0 within 30 days.

DO I HAVE TO WRITE THIS BRIEF?

Once aware of these various policy considerations, there are several other preliminary issues that a respondent must evaluate. The most important question of all is whether a brief must be written at all. The following are factors to consider in answering this question.

1. Was The Notice Of Appeal Timely Filed?

Most jurisdictions have time limits concerning how many days a convicted defendant has in which to file a notice of appeal. Failure to file the notice within this time period is normally held to be jurisdictional. An appeal that was not timely filed can be dismissed on respondent's motion. Thus an appellate prosecutor must consult the local court rules or codes and determine under the particular procedural posture of the case just how long the appellant had to file the notice and whether or not it was timely filed. It is true that most clerks' offices in the lower courts notice and reject notices that are filed beyond the time limits. But, experience teaches that sometimes such maters elude their identification.

Respondent also needs to ascertain how the days in the time period are calculated. Some jurisdictions count only court days while others count every calendar day. Some jurisdictions count the first day while others exclude it. Counsel should also determine how the jurisdiction handles situations where the last day for filing falls on a Saturday or Sunday. Most jurisdictions call for filing on the next court day, but a few require filing on the preceding court day.

It must be remembered that many states have adopted the prison-mailbox rule and hold that when an inmate mails a document to the court, it is presumed filed on the day it is given to the prison authorities for mailing. Normally the penal institutions place a date on the envelope indicating when the institution received it.

Even if the notice of appeal was not filed in time, the appellate court may nevertheless have methods allowing it to proceed with the appeal.

Recognizing the possible harsh result of arbitrary time limits, some courts have developed the doctrine of "constructive notice of appeal." When a defendant has done all that he can do to file the notice and has relied upon the assurances of trial counsel that the notice would be timely filed, but did not do so, the courts held that either there was a timely constructive filing or allowed a belated filing and held that the defendant should not be penalized by the failings of the attorney.

Where the notice is not timely filed, appellate prosecutor should never assume there was such constructive notice. Respondent should make a motion to dismiss and thereby force the defendant to make a showing sufficient to satisfy the appellate court.

2. Is The Notice Of Appeal Sufficient?

Some states require that the notice of appeal be only very general while others require great specificity. The notice should be examined to determine if it meets the court's requirements.

3. Where Is The Defendant?

Perhaps the most demoralizing event for an appellate prosecutor is to complete a long and difficult respondent's brief only to learn that the defendant either died months earlier or escaped. Obviously, if the appellant has died either from natural causes or as the result of prison violence, the appeal is moot and should be dismissed or abated. Respondent cannot rely upon appellant's counsel to make such notification because often in appellate matters there is little or no contact between an appellant and her counsel.

Most jurisdictions will not allow an appellant who is a jail or prison escapee to have the benefit of the judicial system's review. The underlying theory is that because the fugitive has voluntarily and intentionally absented himself from the jurisdiction of the court, he is not entitled to any benefit or protection from the court.

Thus, the appellate prosecutor needs to contact the proper correctional authorities and make certain the appellant is still alive and in custody. In some states, procedures are in place whereby the prison automatically notifies the prosecutor's office of deaths or escapes.

However, in larger jurisdictions with numerous prisons, the system does not exist or is unreliable. There is no substitute for the appellate prosecutor picking up the phone and ascertaining the status of the defendant.

4. Has The Issue Already Been Resolved?

It may not be necessary to do extensive research and writing on an issue if the issue has already been presented to and resolved by the appellate court. Often co-perpetrators will end up being charged and prosecuted separately. By the time you get your appeal, the co-perpetrator's appeal may have already been heard and resolved by the appellate court. A careful advocate will research the status of any co-perpetrator's case to avoid researching and writing the issue again. Of course such prior rulings would not qualify under the law-of-the-case doctrine, but the analysis of the appellate court in the prior case should prove persuasive. In some jurisdictions, it may be possible for the respondent's counsel to actually cite the prior appeal. Counsel needs to check the local rules on this point.

5. Does The Brief Comply With The Local Rules?

Every jurisdiction has a set of rules to which every appellant's opening brief must conform. Sometimes the quality of the opening brief may be so bad that a motion to strike may be appropriate. Many of the rules deal with highly technical matters such as where to place the case numbers. But, other rules are more important, such as the requirement that there be a detailed procedural statement reciting the important events in the case or the requirement that a statement of facts shows the evidence adduced below with proper citations to the record. Such a statement is to present, in the light most favorable to the judgment of the trier of fact, the events constituting the crime. Often, the appellant's statement of facts may be so bad, or so lacking in citations to the record, that a motion to strike may be in order.

On the other hand, by not making the motion to dismiss, a respondent (appellee) has a wonderful opportunity to present a detailed, proper statement of facts, to gain additional credibility with the court and to make opposing counsel look lazy or inept. Thus, the decision on how to handle such a rule-breaking appellant's brief is a tactical question dependant on the situation and the philosophy of the appellate court. This is a variation on the earlier admonition to know you court. Some appellate courts demand precise compliance with the rules regarding statements of fact, other take a less stringent view. In any event, the issue must be considered by the advocate facing a decidedly inept opening brief.

If the brief is really atrocious, both on the facts and the law, the appellate prosecutor needs to be aware of another issue. If the brief is sufficiently inept, the appellate prosecutor must seriously consider a motion to dismiss now or face ineffective assistance claims in habeas. It does little good to win the appeal now just to face habeas petitions questioning appellate counsel's conduct. It may be better to force counsel to submit a better brief, or be replaced by new counsel, than to be involved in habeas corpus litigation in state and federal court for the next decade.

DO YOU HAVE THE RECORD YOU NEED?

In some jurisdictions, the filing of the notice of appeal triggers a duty on the part of the trial court or the clerk to produce and transmit a record of the relevant proceedings to the appellate court. In other jurisdictions, it is the responsibility of the appellant or both the appellant and the respondent. Regardless of which procedure is utilized by your state, you must make certain that you have all of the relevant reporter's transcripts. For example, when the appellant claims that the trial court erred in imposing sanctions on the defense by barring defense witness because there had been a failure by the defense to comply with state discovery rules and claims that the court erred by not considering lesser sanctions, it would be essential for the respondent to have a copy of the reporter's transcript of the hearing at which the court considered the discovery violation and imposed the sanctions.

The method of obtaining the needed transcript will vary from jurisdiction to jurisdiction. In some states a motion to augment the record must be filed with the appellate court. In other jurisdictions, counsel for respondent has the obligation to obtain the transcript and file it with the court. Whatever the local procedure is, counsel must ensure that the relevant material is provided to the appellate court.

When faced with a situation where the appellant has failed to provide a needed transcript, it is tempting to simply take the position that it was the appellant's burden to provide it. He has failed in that burden and thus has failed to meet the burden of proving error by the lower court, and, therefore, the appellant must lose the issue on appeal. While such an approach may prevail in a conservative appellate court, it will simply set up a claim of ineffectiveness of counsel on appeal at the next tier of the appellate courts.

This is precisely what happened in *People v. Barton,* 21 Cal.3d 513 (1978). At the intermediate appellate court counsel for the appellant raised an issue regarding the trial court's denial of a motion to suppress evidence. The respondent took the position that because there was no transcript of the suppression motion in the record, the appellant had failed to meet his burdens or presentation or persuasion. While this view prevailed in the intermediate appellate court, the California Supreme Court quickly determined that the failure to produce the record amounted to ineffective assistance of appellate counsel. They reversed the judgment of the intermediate appellate court because of ineffective assistance of appellate counsel and ordered the matter remanded to the intermediate court with orders to augment the record with the missing transcript and then decide the case on the merits.

Thus, an advocate must recognize that in those situations where the essence of the respondent's entire argument is that the appellant has totally failed to fulfill his or her burden of producing the record, what appears to be the shortest route to an affirmance, may in fact be a mirage. It may actually be the start of long collateral attacks on the competency of counsel.

LOOK FOR STATE PROCEDURAL BARS

Before an appellant can raise an issue with the state appellate court, he must first clear a number of hurdles. Numerous state rules may be invoked to preclude the appellate court from reaching the merits of an appellant's claim.

1. Standing

An appellant will try to raise an issue that she lacks standing to raise. For example, she may be trying to raise a search and seizure issue when she lacks the standing to raise the claim, e.g., a burglar caught in the act may not complain that the police failed to give proper knock and notice at the victim's home before entering it.

2. Failure To Object

Failure to object is perhaps the most often violated principle of appellate law. In order to raise an objection on appeal, the appellant must have made an objection in the trial court.

3. Timeliness And Specificity

The objection must have been made in a timely manner and must have been on the same grounds being raised in the appellate court. Normally the raising of one ground in the trial court does not allow the raising of a different objection to the same evidence on appeal.

4. Bad Faith

In an era of ever increasing legal sophistication by some defendants, appellate lawyers are confronted more and more with defendants playing one constitutional right off against another. Often the game is played so obviously that a claim of bad faith by the appellant can be made on appeal

5. Invited Error

At trial a criminal defendant will invite or suggest that the court take a particular action. That defendant cannot then claim error on appeal when he had invited the action that is now attacked. Some states add a requirement that the actions of defense counsel must have a clear tactical purpose or so state on the record for suggesting the particular action. In any event, whenever possible an appellate prosecutor should be aware of, and use, this issue.

6. Mootness

The appellant may attempt to raise an issue that has become moot. Mootness occurs when there is no possible relief that an appellate court can render to the appellant. For example, if a defendant was complaining about certain terms and conditions of probation, the issue would be moot if, in another case a few weeks later he had been convicted and was serving a prison term. There is no possible relief that an appellate court could give because, regardless of its ruling, the appellant would still be in prison.

PROTECTING YOUR RECORD FROM FUTURE FEDERAL HABEAS CORPUS ATTACKS

With the ever increasing numbers of federal habeas corpus petitions being filed in federal courts, respondent's counsel has to be particularly concerned with state procedural bars. Under federal law, the federal court will not reach the merits of a claim in a habeas petition if the state court has found a state procedural bar exists that precluded the state court from reaching the merits of the appellant's argument.

The state bar must be a state procedural rule that is firmly established and regularly followed. Thus, whenever an appellate prosecutor finds a state procedural bar may exist in a state case, it should be asserted so as to preclude subsequent federal intervention into the merits of the case.
The state decision must rest on a state law ground that is independent of the federal question and adequate to support the decision.[1]

Among the procedural bars that exist are timeliness, the failure to object in the trial court and raising an issue that could have been brought in an earlier direct appeal.

FINDING-THE-REAL-ISSUE STRATEGY

Do not be misled by the appellant's opening brief. Frequently, while the argument is couched in certain terms, the real issue is elsewhere. For example, an argument that the trial court failed to consider certain factors in making its decision on a sentencing question is often little more than a clumsy plea asking that the appellate court re-weigh the evidence on appeal. This, of course, would be improper. In other cases, the claim has been made that the prosecution improperly removed persons who were Jewish. But since no questions had ever been asked about religious beliefs, nor could they in most jurisdictions, the claim became little more than a claim that the prosecution removed individuals who "looked Jewish" or had "Jewish sounding names." Because neither of these are cognizable classes for *Batson* purposes, the argument was easily refuted. Thus often a respondent's brief is much more persuasive by analyzing and responding to the actual issue rather than the smoke screen created by the appellant.

FINDING-THE-FLAW STRATEGY

It is critically important to look for the flaw in the appellant's argument. In a sense, an appellant's argument is like a house of cards. In order to refute the presumption of regularity that attaches to every judgment, the appellant must assemble persuasive facts, law and logic. If there is a flaw in any of these sections, the entire house of cards will crumble.

In looking for the flaw, the first step is to have fully read the record. Make sure the appellant's statement of facts and later use of those facts is absolutely accurate. Often an appellant's argument can only be made by distorting the facts or omitting significant events. Care must be given to this issue because often the factual premise of the appellant's argument is either wrong or incomplete. Showing this flaw will normally undercut the appellant's position.

If the appellant has managed to give an accurate factual presentation, then check the legal analysis. Often important legal authorities are missing. For example, one appellant argued that a single erroneous question by the prosecutor about a post-*Miranda* statement constituted reversible *Doyle* error. The argument initially seemed logical and persuasive, until it was determined that the research omitted the one United States Supreme Court case on point and directly contrary to appellant's position.[2]

In other cases, the appellant's logic is flawed. For example, simply because the defense counsel was disbarred at the time of trial, it does not follow that counsel rendered ineffective representation when the disbarment was because the payment for bar dues it turned out had been lost in the mail. In other situations, the answer may be that simply because error existed, it does not mean it was reversible error.

FINALLY, WHAT IS THE PRAYER FOR RELIEF?

Often, an appellant with a winning issue will try to obtain more relief than the appellant is entitled to have. Always carefully examine the requested relief. Is the appellant entitled to the specific relief that is being requested? For instance, an appellant who has shown he is entitled to a partial re-sentencing on an allegation of certain priors will ask instead, for an entire new sentencing hearing. In other cases, appellants who have shown they may be entitled to a hearing on a limited issue will ask for a de novo hearing on all related issues. It is important to pay particular attention what relief is being sought.

ENDNOTES

[1] *Coleman v. Thompson*, 501 U.S. 722, 731-732, 111 S.Ct. 2546, 115 L.Ed.2d 640 (1991).

[2] *Greer v. Miller*, 483 U.S. 756, 97 L.Ed.2d 618, 107 S. Ct. 3102 (1987).

SEVEN

RESEARCH RESOURCES:
An Appellate Lawyer's Tools Of The Trade

DONALD J. ZELENKA
ASSISTANT DEPUTY ATTORNEY GENERAL
SOUTH CAROLINA ATTORNEY GENERAL'S OFFICE
COLUMBIA, SOUTH CAROLINA

The acquisition of knowledge is the mission of research, the transmission of knowledge is the mission of teaching and the application of knowledge is the mission of public service.

James A. Perkins (1911-1998), President, Cornell University

An appellate prosecutor has many available resources to ensure that the presentation to the court complies with the applicable court procedures. The appellate lawyer must use these tools to persuade the court of the soundness of its position. The written presentation should have sound structure, appropriate length, clarity and continuity. The following resources should provide the appellate prosecutor with assistance in these presentations.

ASSISTANCE FOR THE APPELLATE PROSECUTOR
NDAA, APRI, NAAG, AGACL, NYPTI AND CJLF

Prosecutor and attorney general associations are excellent research resources. In essence, they provide added manpower without the costs—fellow prosecutors helping each other.

1. The National District Attorneys Association (NDAA)
http://www.ndaa-apri.org/

The National District Attorney Association (NDAA) was formed in 1950 as the "National Association of County and Prosecuting Attorneys" in response to the growth of crime and the increasing demand for community protection. The association's current name was adopted in 1959. During the same year, the association qualified as a nonprofit, tax-exempt institution for the purpose of receiving tax-free contributions and grants. NDAA is the largest national professional organization specifically serving the needs of prosecutors in the United States. NDAA represents the interests of prosecutors from major metropolitan areas as well as rural communities.

NDAA influences public policy affecting the safety of America's communities by advocating prosecutorial views through contacts with the White House, Congress, U.S. Department of Justice and other government agencies. Today, NDAA offers local prosecutors the opportunity to network with fellow prosecutors throughout the nation to enhance their knowledge, skills and influence.

NDAA provides these publications:

- *National Prosecution Standards.* $15.00. Published in 1991, this is the second edition of this book. The standards are recommended guidelines concerning many aspects of a prosecutor's office.
- *Trial Technique Predicate Questions.* $25.00. Revised for the first time since its original publication in 1977. A sampling of predicate questions to help improve a prosecutor's trial technique by getting evidence admitted in trial.

- *The Prosecutor's Deskbook: Ethical and Emerging Issues for 21st Century Prosecutors—3rd Edition. $50.00.* The Prosecutor's Deskbook is available again (for the first time since 1977), in a new and revised format. Written by prosecutors for prosecutors, it is designed to educate prosecutors about today's difficult and challenging ethical dilemmas and potentially troublesome courtroom issues. It discusses concerns such as the successful prosecution of shaken-baby and vehicular homicides cases, cyber crime and cyber stalking, countering attacks on the reliability of your eyewitness identifications, navigating the intricacies of police-shooting and civil rights liability cases and techniques for successful media relations.

2. American Prosecutors Research Institute (APRI)

In 1984, the National District Attorneys Association founded the American Prosecutors Research Institute (APRI) as a non-profit research and program development resource for prosecutors at all levels of government. Since that time, APRI has become a vital national clearinghouse of information on the prosecutorial function. The Institute is committed to providing interdisciplinary responses to the complex problems of criminal justice.

It is also committed to supporting the highest professional standards among officials entrusted with the awesome responsibility for public safety. Today's prosecutors are expected to have a sophisticated understanding of social violence, medical and scientific advances, media relations and community development. The institute has assembled programs and a staff who meet these demands.

The Institute has developed particular areas of expertise, and prosecutors with problems and needs in those areas can contact the Institute.

Child Abuse, Abduction and Exploitation—Parental kidnapping and stranger abduction, neglect, physical and sexual abuse, fatalities, interviewing skills, computer-facilitated sexual exploitation, and prostitution and trafficking.

Community Prosecution—Community-oriented prosecution addresses the needs of specific neighborhoods by developing proactive, innovative legal strategies and helping create partnerships that will provide long-term solutions to neighborhood livability issues.

DNA Forensics—Scientific, legal, and trial advocacy issues at both a basic and advanced level, including STRs, Mitochondrial DNA, Y-Chromosome Typing, CODIS, and non-human DNA.

Juvenile Justice—Training for newly assigned juvenile prosecutors and rural prosecutors, balanced and restorative justice, DMC, leadership summits, and serious and violent offenders.

Research—Caseload/workload studies, performance measures, program evaluations, policy analyses, identification of promising practices in hate crimes, drug prevention/intervention, and victim/witness assistance.

Traffic Law—Impaired driving issues such as HGN, DRE, toxicology, crash reconstruction, vehicular homicide, and breath testing instruments, and general consulting services.

Violence Against Women—Domestic violence, including cultural and immigration issues, rural issues, sexual assault, stalking and cyber stalking.

Violent Crime Initiatives—On May 14, 2001, President Bush announced Project Safe Neighborhoods (PSN), a partnership between local prosecutors and their federal counterparts and attendant law enforcement agencies aimed at reducing gun violence. was formed to specifically address the issues arising from this new initiative.

White Collar Crime—Telemarketing fraud, Internet fraud, identity theft, insurance fraud, and similar crimes.

3. National Association Of Attorneys General Association (NAAG) www.naag.org

The Association maintains an office on Capitol Hill in Washington, D.C. (750 First Street, N.E., Suite 1100, Washington, D.C. 20002, phone: 202-326-6000, fax: 202-408-7014). There are numerous working groups managed by assistant attorneys general that provide assistance on briefs, and amicus curiae matters. The Association working groups will also hold conference calls to assist and advise on current legal trends. The working groups include criminal procedure, habeas corpus, state constitutional law, election law, and other various issues that attorneys general face in their jobs.

4. Association Of Government Attorneys In Capital Litigation (AGACL)

AGACL is a group of state and federal trial and appellate prosecutors involved in homicide trials and appeals where the death penalty is sought. This organization began in 1980 as a response to the organized litigation effort against the death penalty that overwhelmed the limited manpower of attorneys handling the state litigation in the earlier cases. The group's mission is to train prosecutors in the specialized area of capital litigation at the trial, appeal and federal habeas corpus level and act as a clearinghouse of ideas and information in this area. The group has an annual training conference in the summer. An annual summer conference provides updates on current court trends in capital litigation. The conference also provides technical training on trial and appellate advocacy in death penalty matters. AGACL has a current website www.agacl.org. The website allows for registration for the conference.

The Association will provide contacts for assistance in capital appeals and issues. Regional vice-presidents are elected annually with the responsibility to maintain contact and communication with the capital litigators in their areas.

The Association is also involved with the New York Prosecution Training Institute (NYPTI) in preparing an expert witness bank. The address is NYPTI, 150 State Street , 5th Floor, Albany, New York 12207. (518–432–1100).

5. The Criminal Justice Legal Foundation (CJLF)

The Criminal Justice Legal Foundation is a nonprofit public interest law organization dedicated to restoring a balance between the rights of crime victims and the criminally accused. The Foundation's purpose is to assure that people who are guilty of committing crimes receive swift and certain punishment in an orderly and thoroughly constitutional manner.

To accomplish this, CJLF attorneys introduce persuasive legal arguments in criminal cases before the state and federal appellate courts to encourage precedent-setting decisions which recognize the constitutional rights of victims and law-abiding society. The Foundation's scholarly, low-profile approach has resulted in several United States Supreme Court decisions having a national effect to reduce the length, complexity and expense of appeals, recognize the rights and needs of child crime victims, and improve law enforcement's ability to identify and prosecute drug manufacturers and traffickers. The address is Criminal Justice Legal Foundation, Post Office Box 1199, Sacramento, CA 95812. The Internet Webpage that includes articles and briefs is http://www.cjlf.org/

INTERNET LEGAL RESEARCH AND RESOURCES FOR THE APPELLATE PROSECUTOR

1. Basic Legal Search Engines

These internet research tools are not as user-friendly as Westlaw and Lexis-Nexis, but they provide an alternative. This may be necessary when funding is at issue or there is unavailability of the subscription services

- Findlaw—www.findlaw.com—Findlaw allows for limited search under court opinion names, dates and summaries. It also provides information in practice areas.
- Loislaw—www.loislaw.com—Fee-based Loislaw publishes case law, statutory law, constitutions, administrative law, court rules, and other authority for all 50 states and D.C. plus the 18 most important Federal law libraries. All Loislaw law libraries are exact duplications of the official law.

2. United States Supreme Court Decisions

The official website is www.supremecourtus.gov This website answers many demands of its practitioners. The website provides day-of-decision access to opinions, docket status information and orders. Transcripts of recent oral arguments are also available for viewing on this website. The following sites are also useful to the prosecutor with a case headed to the Supreme Court.

- Supreme Court Decisions since 1990—http://supct.law.cornell.edu/supct/index.html—The website is maintained by Cornell Law School. Opinions on the day of decision can be downloaded in either Adobe PDF or html formats. In addition, the website has areas that describe pending cases before the Court. It also has archived recent decisions in useful topic areas for study.

- Abstracts and Oral Arguments—www.oyez.org—This site provides the audio of recent oral arguments and the simultaneous viewing of the written transcripts. As a training tool, this site provides an outstanding tool, showing what is the highest quality—advocates present their best prepared arguments and the questioning is by the highly prepared jurists. In preparation for an argument, this resource provides a unique view into an issue which may impact upon the advocates handling of future cases.

- American Bar Association Supreme Court Preview—This website provides online access to merits briefs and commentary on pending cases to be argued. This site is located at http://www.abanet.org/publiced/preview/home.html.

- Washington Post Supreme Court Website—Searchable archive of Associated Press and Washington Post staff articles on the Supreme Court. This website can be found at: http://www.washingtonpost.com/wp-dyn/nation/courts/supremecourt.

3. Federal Circuit Case Sites

Each federal circuit has developed websites which vary in content, but essentially provide access to recently decided cases within days of the opinion. The websites also provide access to background information of the particular members of the court. Additional information includes oral argument schedules, access to briefs and docket information. It also provides information about Circuit Court rules and forms necessary for practice before each court. Some courts, such as the Eighth Circuit, provide audio of oral arguments.

- First Circuit—www.law.emory.edu/1circuit
  http://www.ca1.uscourts.gov/main.htm
- Second Circuit—www.tourolaw.edu/2ndCircuit
  http://www.ca2.uscourts.gov/
- Third Circuit—http://www.ca3/
- Fourth Circuit—http://www.ca4.uscourts.gov/
- Fifth Circuit—http://www.ca5.uscourts.gov/
- Sixth Circuit—http://pacer.ca6.uscourts.gov/opinions/main.php
- Seventh Circuit—http://www.ca7.uscourts.gov/
- Eighth Circuit—http://www.ca8.uscourts.gov/opinions/opinions.html
  http://8cc-www.ca8.uscourts.gov/Oral-Arg/scripts/GetOralArg.asp
- Ninth Circuit—http://www.ca9.uscourts.gov
- Tenth Circuit—http://www.ck10.uscourts.gov
  http://www.kscourts.org/ca10/
- Eleventh Circuit—www.law.emory.edu/11circuit/index.html
  http://www.ca11.uscourts.gov/opinions/opinions.html
- D.C. Circuit—http://www.cadc.uscourts.gov
- Federal Circuit—http://www.fedcir.gov/

4. PACER Website–http://pacer.psc.uscourts.gov/

Public Access to Court Electronic Records (PACER) is an electronic public access service that allows users to obtain case and docket information from Federal Appellate, District and Bankruptcy courts, and from the U.S. Party/Case Index. In some courts, it provides access to all filed documents, orders, affidavits and transcripts in a format that can be downloaded to the user.

5. State Court Decisions—http://www.ncsconline.org/D_KIS/info_court_web_sites.html#state

The National Center for State Courts Website provides the most up-to-date links to the evolving state court websites. These websites can be extremely useful as a resource to the appellate lawyer. Most appellate court sites provide background information on the individual members of the court, the appellate rules, forms and orders. Some websites include access to briefs filed on the appellate court. This NCSC website compiles both appellate court and trial court materials in each state.

A recent trend in some websites, such as the Florida state court website, (http://wfsu.org/gavel2gavel/) is to provide real-time and archived audio and video of appellate arguments and access to briefs, in addition to the reported decisions. These websites can provide excellent training for the appellate advocate. By studying the actual arguments, a lawyer can learn what works and what does not work with the court. The appellate advocate can also study what opposing counsel has done in the past before the court in her arguments, such as whether she saves her best for reply rather than a closer in her opening argument. Even if your court website does not provide video or audio recordings of oral arguments, other states websites can still be used to assist in preparation and study of appellate advocacy.

Each appellate advocate should regularly access their own state court website to ensure an accurate understanding of relevant court rules, to provide a daily update of opinions, and to learn about scheduled oral arguments. Some courts, such as South Carolina, present a brief synopsis of issues pending oral arguments on its docket.

6. Constitutional And Statutory Sites

These sites include interesting and useful information for the advocate:

- The U.S. Constitution—http://www.house.gov/Constitution/Constitution.html

- The U.S. Code—http://www4.law.cornell.edu/uscode/ Or http://uscode.house.gov/usc.htm
- Federal Rules of Evidence—http://www.law.cornell.edu/rules/fre/overview.html
- Federal Rules of Civil Procedure (1998)—http://www.law.cornell.edu/rules/frcp/

7. Other Useful Legal and Non-legal Websites

- Court TV Online—www.courttv.com/
- Citation Guide for Lawyers—www.law.cornell.edu/citation/citation.table.html
- Court Rules—www.llrx.com/columns/litigat.htm
- Legal Ethics Information—http://www.legalethics.com/
- The Code of Hammurabi—http://www.fordham.edu/halsall/ancient/hamcode.html
- Webster's Revised Unabridged Dictionary 1913—http://humanities.uchicago.edu/forms_unrest/webster.form.html
- Roget's Thesaurus—http://humanities.uchicago.edu/forms_unrest/ROGET.html
- Bartlett's Quotations—http://www.columbia.edu/acis/bartleby/bartlett/

8. Appellate Web Blogs

These blogs provide excellent information in appellate practice areas created by individuals extraordinarily interested in this practice area - a must for starting each morning of appellate work.

- *SCOTUSBlog*—http://www.goldsteinhowe.com/blog/index.cfm—This blog is dedicated to Supreme Court practice and discussions. This site is updated throughout each day with information and commentary related to recent and future decisions by the court.

- *How Appealing* BLOG—http://legalaffairs.org/howappealing/ —This blog is more general in news and commentary and reviews trends in all courts on hot appellate topics. Recently associated with Legal Affairs Magazine, it was launched in May 2002 by Howard Bashman due to a dirth of appellate law websites. Like *SCOTUSBlog*, it is updated throughout the day. This blog expands its commentary beyond the United States Supreme Court to include state and federal appellate courts. The blog links to newspaper articles throughout the nation which addressing issues related to appellate practice and decisions. A monthly feature is "20 Questions for an Appellate Judge" where various appellate court judges are asked questions, including advice on appellate advocacy.

- *Appellate.Net*—http://www.appellate.net/—Mayer, Brown, Rowe & Maw LLP's Appellate and Supreme Court Practice website. This site has collected information and links relevant to Supreme Court and appellate practice. The site also has information about their attorneys and the cases handled in recent years by the firm in the United States Supreme Court.

9. Palm Pilot Support Legal Websites

If you have a palm handheld PDA and need to find a better use for it, these websites may be the answer. They may provide you needed advice on useful software to make your life easier and the PDA more useful.

- JurisPDA@nyls.edu—The New York Law School developed this website with the users of PalmPilots in mind. There is a strong case to be made for finding a way to put an enormous amount of information at the fingertips of lawyers who may not always have their laptop with them. Working through New York Law School's Center for Professional Values and Practice, the school developed an innovative website that would make it fast and easy for the growing legions of professionals who use Palm Powered handhelds to access and download important legal information and resources. Designed especially for Palm handheld users, the Website enables practicing attorneys and legal scholars to organize and manage legal data more efficiently than was ever before possible. Instead of having to carry pounds of bulky books and reference materials, law students and others can simply download the information they need onto their Palm Powered handhelds via a HotSync® operation and pop the small, lightweight computer into a pocket, backpack or briefcase for access at a moment's notice.

The website has gathered an inventory of the most useful Palm OS® handheld applications for lawyers. In addition to essential legal reference materials—the U.S. Constitution, Federal Rules of Evidence and selected U.S. Supreme Court cases, for example—the site includes applications that allow users to create their own flashcards and quizzes, turning the handheld computer into a tool that lets students study anytime.

To help users improve time-management skills—critical to success for professionals—there are links to applications that assist users in maintaining a schedule and staying on top of the many demands of legal practice.

The JurisPDA website further extends the many benefits lawyers may already enjoy from using a Palm Powered handheld computer. For example, users with wireless-enabled handhelds can conduct online research and search legal-information databases, such as Westlaw, from anywhere they have wireless coverage. Lawyers may also find the PalmOS handheld computer, along with the Palm Portable Keyboard, to be a very convenient tool for taking notes right in class or while studying in the law library. There are a number of programs that let Palm Powered handheld users print documents directly from their handheld to any printer with an infrared (IR) port.

- pdaJD.com Website—www.pdaJD.com—Another website devoted to Palm and Pocket PC devices and lawyers. This site provides reviews of recent software, general articles and access to law related documents. Like JurisPDA, pdaJD.com provides advice and information for lawyer users.

THE ESSENTIAL REFERENCE SHELF FOR THE APPELLATE ADVOCACTE

Available to appellate advocates are many style manuals, self-help books and other written materials to assist them in their legal writing and court presentations. The following books are generally available at bookstores or over the internet.

1. Manuals For The Appellate Advocate.

Without a doubt, the most useful manual for appellate practice is Stern and Gressman, *Supreme Court Practice: For Practice in the Supreme Court of the United States*, 8th ed. (2001) BNA Books. ($395.00). This is the Bible of Supreme Court practice. It is a must have for any appellate advocate because not only does it give the necessary tips for practice before the Supreme Court of the United States, it is an excellent resource for general appellate practice within its covers. This book covers all aspects of the practice from certiorari petitions to where to stand in the courtroom. This Edition updates the recent Rule changes in the Court.

The Court Rules—Every appellate advocate must have ready access to the applicable rules of court for the particular jurisdiction. This is a must and the failure to review the rules can be critical to the success of the case.

Style Manuals—Every law office and governmental law firm should adopt a single style manual as its "bible" and follow it consistently.

- William A. Sabin, *The Gregg Reference Manual* (8th ed. 1996) (Glencoe/McGraw—Hill). This is a widely used manual. It covers punctuation, capitalization, numbers, abbreviations, plurals and possessives, spelling, compound words, word division, grammar and usage.
- *The Chicago Manual of Style* (14th ed. 1993) (The University of Chicago Press). This book is the old standby, dating from 1906. It is probably used more by academics, however, than the legal and business community.

- Texas Law Review, *Manual on Usage & Style* (9th ed. 2002) (TLR Ass'n). This pocket-sized reference contains the rules for resolving most of the grammar, punctuation, word usage, and style questions that the average lawyer faces. Any book that is endorsed by Charles Alan Wright must have something going for it.

2. Criminal Law Treatises And Manuals Useful To The Appellate Practitioner

- *Georgetown Law Journal Annual Criminal Procedure Project.* The Georgetown Law Journal annually publishes the Project which summarizes in a very readable and accessible format critical criminal procedure decisions in the Supreme Court and Courts of Appeals. It is found in most appellate judge's offices. It can be ordered as a single issue from The Georgetown Law Journal Association, 600 New Jersey Avenue, N.W., Washington, D.C. 20001.

- Leibman and Hertz, *Federal Habeas Corpus Practice and Procedure*, (Michie 4th Edition 2001) A two volume set of the authors interpretation on federal habeas corpus litigation. This is considered by many habeas practitioners on both the prosecution and defense to be the definitive treatise for use in this area. This work is available in either print or CD-Rom. The publisher describes the treatise as follows: "*Federal Habeas Corpus Practice and Procedure* stands alone as the authoritative and practical treatise for achieving habeas corpus relief in both capital and non-capital cases. It is the resource cited most frequently by the U.S. Supreme Court and lower federal courts, as well as by thousands of other attorneys who practice in habeas corpus proceedings."

- *The Federal Habeas Corpus Game—Instructional Manual,* California Department of Justice. The California Attorney General's office form book and procedural manual for federal habeas corpus. This work is excellent assistance to other governmental offices in their approach to this area. A contact person in the California Attorney General's Office for this information is Dane R. Gillette, Senior Assistant Attorney General, 50 Fremont Street, Suite 300, San Francisco, California 94105-2239 (415-356-6202).

- *The Dictionary of In-com-pe-tence—Responding to Claims of Ineffective Assistance,* California Department of Justice. This is an excellent compilation of caselaw summaries of numerous ineffective assistance decisions from the various federal circuits. The work outlines specific claims and how the courts treat them. A contact person in the California Attorney General's Office for this information is Dane R. Gillette, Senior Assistant Attorney General, 50 Fremont Street, Suite 300, San Francisco, California 94105-2239 (415-356-6202).

3. Brief Writing Aids

The following books are dedicated to appellate brief writing:

- *The Winning Brief; 100 Tips for Persuasive Briefing in Trial and Appellate Court* by Bryan A. Garner ($45.00) Hardcover, 468 pages (1999) Oxford University Press. These are Garner's practical tips developed from his brief-writing seminars. His tips are checklists for the development of a persuasive style necessary to maximize your position before the court.

- Edward D. Re, *Brief Writing and Oral Argument,* Oceana 5th ed. (1983). This book originally appeared in 1951 and has become a classic. The focus of the book is on the content of an appellate brief and the strategies of effective persuasion.

- Girvan Peck, *Writing Persuasive Briefs* (1984) (Little, Brown). This book serves as a nice compliment to the Re book, because its emphasis is more on the linguistic aspects of persuasive writing.

- Thomas R. Haggard, *Legal Drafting in a Nutshell* (1996) (West). This book covers the process and the techniques for drafting both pleading documents and legislation.

- Bryan A. Garner, *Garner's Redbook Manual of Legal Style* (2002). The Redbook provides a comprehensive guide to the essential rules of legal writing. Unlike most style or grammar guides, it focuses on the special needs of legal writers, answering a wide spectrum of questions about grammar and style – both rules as well as exceptions. The Redbook also gives detailed, authoritative advice on punctuation, capitalization, spelling, footnotes, and citations, with illustrations in legal context. Designed for law students, law professors, practicing lawyers and judges, the work emphasizes the ways in which legal writing differs from other styles of technical writing. The how-to sections deal with editing and proofreading, numbers and symbols, and overall document design.

- Seattle University School of Law Legal Writing Institute. http://www.lwionline.org This law school website contains forums on legal writing. It is primarily for law school educators but it has constructive ideas on writing.

4. General Legal Writing Manuals

These manuals can assist a writer to apply a persuasive style to the pleading. Each has tools to structure an argument in plain language.

- *The Elements of Legal Style* by Bryan A. Garner ($27.50) Hardcover—236 pages (1991) Oxford Univ Pr (Trade). Garner's writing and style guide utilizes the format of Strunk & White's classic book, *The Elements of Style*. This work contains numerous examples of clear writing from noted legal authors, including Oliver Wendell Holmes.

- Bryan A. Garner, *A Dictionary of Modern Legal Usage* (1987) (Oxford University Press). No serious legal writer should be without this book. Many appellate judges refer to this work extensively.

- Richard C. Wydick, *Plain English for Lawyers* (4th ed. 1998) (Carolina Academic Press). ($10.95) This is truly a classic. It is a concise book which covers all the basic principles of good legal writing. The book also contains useful exercises in each chapter. These exercises can be done as refreshers on effective writing.

- Morton S. Freeman, *The Practical Lawyer* (1979), and James D. Maugans, *The Grammatical Lawyer II* (1996) (ALI-ABA). These books contain reprints of the writing column that has appeared in *The Practical Lawyer* since 1976. The primary focus is on word usage, but the books also address some of the more common grammar, punctuation, and syntax problems that the legal writer faces. They have excellent indexes.

- Edward Good, *Mightier Than The Sword-Powerful Writing In The Legal Profession* (1989) (Blue Jeans Press). The author condenses good legal writing to nineteen rules and explains each of them in detail. The author is a proponent of plain, concise, comprehensible legal writing.

- Thomas R. Haggard, *The Lawyer's Book of Rules For Effective Legal Writing* (1996) (Rothmann). This booklet contains more rules (44) than Good's book, but covers them in much less space (26 pages). Designed as a handy desk reference, the booklet also contains a self-editing checklist.

- Tom Goldstein and Jethro Lieberman, *The Lawyer's Guide to Writing Well* (1989) University of California Press. A practical book that outlines the causes and consequences of bad writing and prescribes straightforward remedies.

- David Mellinkoff, *Language of the Law*, Paperback, 1st ed., 544pp. Aspen Law & Business (1973) ($29.00). This book has been described as magisterial, and a book that no lawyer should ignore.

5. The Writer's References

Each writer must have the following books or similar ones within easy reach to be a competent writer and editor.

- **Dictionary**—A comprehensive dictionary, more advanced than the one you had in college, is needed by every writer. One dictionary frequently recommended, but out of print, is the 1987 *Random House Dictionary of the English Language*. Other recommended dictionaries are *The American Heritage Dictionary of the English Language* ($50.00) Hardcover, 3rd ed., 214 pp. Houghton Mifflin (1992) and *Webster's Third New International Dictionary, Unabridged* ($119.00) Hardcover, 2663 pp., Merriam-Webster, Incorporated (January 1993).

- **Thesaurus**—A competent thesaurus aids a writer's struggle to state similar concepts in a persuasive manner. *Roget's International Thesaurus* ($21.00) Hardcover, 5th ed., 1168 pp. HarperCollins Publishers, Inc.(1992), *Roget's II: The New Thesaurus American Heritage* (Retail Price: $45.00) Hardcover, 3rd ed., 1280 pp. Houghton Mifflin Company (1995) and *Webster's New World Thesaurus* (Retail Price: $22.95) Hardcover, 3rd ed. Macmillan Publishing Company, Incorporated (1997) are recommended.

- **Usage book**—An up-to-date language usage book can assist the writer in correcting style errors. *A Dictionary of Modern American Usage*, by Bryan A. Garner (Retail Price: $35.00) Hardcover, 1st ed., 752 pp. Oxford University Press, Incorporated (January 1998) and *The New Fowler's Modern English Usage* , by H. W. Fowler and R. W. Burchfield (Editor) ($25.00) Hardcover, 3rd ed., 864 pp., Oxford University Press, Incorporated (January 1996) are recommended.

- **Grammar Guide**—A basic work on grammar. *The Elements of Grammar* by Margaret D. Shertzer ($9.95) Paperback, 1st ed., 180 pp. Macmillan Publishing Company, Incorporated (1986) is at my fingertips. A recommended in-depth treatment can be found in *Grammar of the English Language (Volumes 1 and 2)* by George O. Curme ($50.00) Hardcover, Verbatim B (1983).

Also recommended for a writer's research shelf are the following types of books.

- *Fowler's Modern English Usage: Dictionary of Modern English Usage* by Henry Watson Fowler ($13.95) Paperback, 2nd ed., 725 pp., Oxford University Press, Incorporated (1983). This is somewhat dated but still authoritative and encyclopedic in range.

- *Style: Toward Clarity and Grace* by Joseph M. Williams, Gregory G. Colomb ($11.00) Paperback, 208 pp., University of Chicago Press (1995). This book is considered to be the best short work on how to achieve clarity in prose.

- *The Elements of Style* by William Strunk and E. B. White (Retail Price: $6.95) Paperback, 3rd ed., 92 pp., Allyn & Bacon, Inc. (1979). This short treatise is provided to all lawyers who become members of the 11th Circuit bar. This book is an essential part of any writer's bookshelf.

- A competent book on editing is useful to the appellate writer. Commentators consider one of the best to be *Line by Line: How to Improve Your Own Writing* by Claire Kehrwald Cook ($8.95) Paperback, 240pp. (Houghton Mifflin Company).

- A standard composition handbook. Commentators recommend these: *The Handbook of Good English* by Edward D. Johnson ($16.00) Paperback, 416 pp., Pocket Books (1991); or *The New Oxford Guide to Writing* by Thomas S. Kane ($14.95) Paperback, 1st ed., 336 pp., Oxford University Press, Incorporated (1994).

6. General Writing Resources

An appellate writer can hit a mental brick wall with writer's block or have style problems due to short-cut boiler plating of arguments to the court. The advocate must always be aware that the goal is to have the document read and considered by the court. If the argument appears in the same language as earlier pleadings, the court may ignore the advocacy that the writer is attempting to present. This is especially a concern for appellate prosecutors who regularly appear before the same court, rather than those who rarely appear. The following resources may assist the writer in breaking such habits and invigorate the advocates writing for the court.

- *On Writing Well: The Classic Guide to Writing Nonfiction* by William Knowlton Zinsser ($14.00) Paperback (320 pages)

6th ed. (1998) HarperReference. A revised and updated edition of one of the most successful guides to writing nonfiction ever published; this is an indispensable tool for a person who writes or wants to learn to write clearly.

- *Woe Is I : The Grammarphobe's Guide to Better English in Plain English* by Patricia T. O'Conner ($11.00) Paperback, 240 pages (1998) Riverhead Books. With delicious wit and a delightfully down-to-earth tone, former New *Times Book Review* editor Patricia O'Conner offers a guide to grammar that teaches you the basics and subtleties of the language—without the kind of jargon that tempted you to cut your high-school English class. Chapter titles include "Comma Sutra" (the joy of punctuation); "Woe Is I" (therapy for pronoun anxiety); "Verbal Abuse" (words on the endangered list), and more.

- *Exercises in Legal Writing Principles by Bryan Garner*. This website provides 50 of Garner's legal writing principles and useful writing exercises related to each principle. The website is http://press-pubs.uchicago.edu/garner/

7. Quotation Books

There may be times when the right thought cannot be uniquely expressed by the writer. At that time referral to a book of quotations may provide a remedy to the writer's woes. The following are books that can be relied upon to address this need.

- David S. Shrager & Elizabeth Frost, *The Quotable Lawyer*, New England Publishing Associates, Inc. (1986). This compilation of quotations from and about lawyers and jurists is very user friendly.

- Fred Shapiro, Comp. *The Oxford Dictionary of American Legal Quotations.* N.Y., Oxford Univ. Press, (1993) This is a collection of not only passages written by judges and legal commentators but also humorous writing from movies, literature and songs concerning the law.

EIGHT

STANDARDS OF REVIEW:
The First Line Of Defense

JAMES F. FLANAGAN
OLIVER ELLSWORTH PROFESSOR OF FEDERAL PRACTICE
UNIVERSITY OF SOUTH CAROLINA SCHOOL OF LAW
COLUMBIA, SOUTH CAROLINA

We are to weigh the competing considerations in such scales as are available.

Justice Benjamin Cardozo, Hoadley v. Hoadley, 244 N.Y. 424, 434 (1927)

When I was an Assistant United States Attorney for the District of Columbia I much preferred trials to appeals. It was apparent to me, as it is to any trial prosecutor who handles their own appeals, that appeals offer the prosecutor little up-side benefit. Once the defendant has been convicted, an appeal can affirm the conviction, but there is the risk of a reversal, retrial and acquittal. Appeals can be disquieting on a personal level. Prosecutors love the courtroom where their trial skills have full play. Research and writing a brief, with its arcane reliance on formality and subtle distinctions is a different forum and much less exciting. I always found that reading a transcript of my trial was a humbling experience. My memory of that devastating cross-examination never was fully confirmed by the reality of the printed page. A cold transcript also reveals missed opportunities and mistakes, which the appellant's brief is also apt to amplify. The experience is similar to hearing your spouse explain exactly *why* you were not the life of the party the previous evening.

An appellate prosecutor, however, is nothing if not resilient, and having overcome obstacles to gain the conviction, now faces the challenge of sustaining the conviction. The appellant's brief defines the issues to which the appellate prosecutor must structure a compelling response. But before gathering all the compelling evidence and decisive precedents, the appellate prosecutor must recognize and utilize the most significant difference between trial and appellate advocacy. Appellate courts do not hear evidence. They are courts of review, and appellate judges must first determine the standard of review to apply to each legal issue on appeal. The standard determines whether appellate review is cursory or detailed. They are the legal terrain on which the issues are deployed and provide greater or less protection to the decisions made below. For the appellate prosecutor they are the first line of defense to many allegations of error.

Legally and practically, standards of review are essential to an effective brief. Legally, they establish the level of deference that the appellate court gives to the decision below. The proper standard defines and limits the appellate court's power to alter the trial decisions. Standards vary on a continuum from those that provide no deference to the trial judge's decision to those that grant substantial deference. At one end, a judge's decision on the law is not entitled to any deference and the reviewing court may decide a legal issue de novo. At the other extreme, a finding of fact by the jury will be overturned only when there is no basis in the record for the jury's decision. Standards of review often specify the evidence considered in reviewing an issue. An error in a jury instruction, for example, is construed in light of the instructions as a whole. The sufficiency of an indictment is determined by the four corners of the document.

As a practical matter, each participant in an appeal has a strong interest in the standard of review. Appellate judges want and need to know the appropriate standard to apply to each issue.[1] They often determine the outcome of the appeal, particularly when a difficult issue is governed by a standard deferential to the trial judge. For advocates, standards of review deferential to the trial judge favor the respondent, automatically creating a heavier burden for the appellant to satisfy before reaching the merits. De novo review favors the appellant because the appellate court has no procedural impediment to reaching the issue and must resolve it.

Most important, standards of review also provide the structure for each argument because they identify the evidence to be reviewed, the factors to be evaluated, their relative importance and the scope of the appellate court's authority. Marshaling all the facts and the substantive law can be done effectively only when the advocate has identified and considered how to satisfy each standard. Each issue must be considered in context of the pertinent standard. Lawyers tend to invoke standards as ritualistic incantations, necessary to appease the appellate gods and legal writing instructors, but to do so ignores the different ways an appellate judge applies the same words to different issues. An appellate court, applying the abuse of discretion standard to the trial judge's limitation of the criminal defendant's cross-examination, which implicates the Constitution, is much less deferential to the trial judge, than when it applies the same standard to a claim that the judge erred in admitting cumulative evidence by the government. Standards cannot be ignored, even if unfavorable. A brief without a standard undermines the credibility of the advocate and allows the opponent, or perhaps worse, the judge's law clerk, to fill the vacuum.

My goal here is to provide an overview of standards of review on direct appeal from criminal convictions. Space precludes a full development of the pertinent standard for each trial ruling. For that I suggest the two volume treatise by Steven Alan Childress and Martha S. Davis, *Federal Standards of Review* (2d ed. 1992). A shorter discussion is found in Michael E. Tigar and Jane B. Tigar, *Federal Appeals, Jurisdiction and Practice* (3rd ed. 1999). There also is a substantial body of commentary on individual standards, such as harmless error and discretionary review in the federal courts.[2] Some articles are devoted to the standards in particular jurisdictions.[3] Those who examine the cited authorities will note my substantial debt to them.[4]

While this chapter primarily focuses on federal standards, there are counterparts in state law. The language of the standards varies from jurisdiction to jurisdiction so care must be taken to establish the correct standard for each court. At best, this chapter is a guide to further research of the precedents in the appellate prosecutor's particular jurisdiction.

ERROR PRESERVATION, PLAIN ERROR AND HARMLESS ERROR

Interlocutory appeals and review of petitions for habeas corpus are beyond the scope of this chapter and those procedures, particularly, federal review of state convictions, have special rules that limit the writ.

The most common mistake in the heat of trial is the failure to properly preserve an error for later appeal. Judges often make critical rulings in sidebar conferences, in-chamber meetings, and off-the-record discussions. Good trial practice mandates that these decisions be placed on the record, but often they are not. The first task is to determine whether each alleged error was properly preserved. Error preservation is not a standard of review, but the rule requiring an objection at trial,[5] (to give the judge an opportunity to correct a mistake immediately), is a fundamental requirement of appellate practice. Generally, an objection to the court's action, or refusal to act, must be made at the time that the court rules, or as soon as the decision is known to counsel. The objection should clearly state the grounds for the objection and the requested action desired by counsel. The generic objections protesting that the evidence is "irrelevant, immaterial and prejudicial" may be insufficiently detailed to preserve the error. More often, objections to the exclusion of evidence may be made without a proffer of the excluded evidence or testimony so there is nothing in the record to establish its relevancy, importance and prejudice to the movant.[6] In some jurisdictions rulings *in limine* are viewed as tentative decisions, and the evidence must be tendered, and objection noted at trial.[7] Finally, the error must be raised in the appellate brief. Appellate courts generally do not consider issues for the first time on appeal. Even those raised may be deemed waived when they are addressed perfunctorily in the brief or oral argument.

Some, but not all,[8] courts may excuse the failure to preserve the error when it rises to the level of plain error. Fed. R. Crim. P. 52(b) provides: "Plain Error. A plain error that affects substantial rights may be considered even though it was not brought to the court's attention."[9] Not every trial error satisfies this exception. There must be an error, which is a deviation from established practice. The error must be "plain" which means that it is clear or obvious under current settled law at the time of trial, or if the settled law has changed after the trial, at the time of the appeal.[10] The error must affect significant rights, which, in the federal system, requires that the appellant establish that the error was prejudicial and affected the outcome of the trial.[11] Once these elements have been established, the appellate court *may* exercise its discretion and consider the issue. The Supreme Court has stated, however, that this discretion should be exercised only when a miscarriage of justice would result or the error affects the fairness, integrity or public reputation of the judicial proceedings. These requirements set a high standard, as seen in the Supreme Court's decisions interpreting the plain error standard. *United States v. Olano*,[12] upheld a conviction although alternate jurors were in the jury room during deliberations. *Johnson v. United States*[13] upheld a conviction although the trial judge improperly withdrew an element of the crime from the jury and decided the issue. A finding that an unpreserved error is not plain, often means that it is deemed a harmless error.

Harmless error is another hurdle the appellant faces, and the appellate prosecutor often uses it. The concept is based upon the fundamental principle that the error can be ignored if it had no impact on the outcome of the trial. This is familiar to every player on the office basketball team as: "No harm no foul."[14] Harmless error applies to constitutional as well as nonconstitutional errors.[15] The constitutional standard is satisfied if the reviewing court finds evidence in the entire record, less the error, supporting a finding of guilty beyond a reasonable doubt.[16] Stated differently, the defendant must establish that, without the error, a directed verdict would have been entered. Generally, the defendant bears the burden of establishing the harm from the error although some errors are so serious that reversal is automatic. Errors affecting the right to counsel or to a fair judge fall into this category.[17]

Harmless error also is found in the Federal Rules of Criminal Procedure[18] and the Federal Rules of Evidence.[19] These standards focus on substantial rights, but most courts examine the impact of the error on the verdict. The Supreme Court articulated the standard in this form:

> "If when all is said and done, the [court's] conviction is sure that the error did not influence the jury, or had but a very

slight effect, the verdict and the judgment should stand.... But if one cannot say, with fair assurance, after pondering all that happened without stripping the erroneous action from the whole, that the judgment was not substantially swayed by the error, it is impossible to conclude that substantial rights were not affected. The inquiry cannot be merely whether there was enough to support the result, apart from the phase affected by the error, it is rather, even so, whether the error itself had substantial influence. If so, if one is left in grave doubt, the conviction cannot stand."[20]

Even though error is established, jurisdictions have different tests measuring the causal connection between the error and its effect on the verdict. These vary from reversing unless the error "probably" did not affect the judgment, to reversing unless it was "highly probable" that the error did not affect the judgment, to a standard that would reverse unless the court finds beyond a reasonable doubt that there was no effect.[21] Many commentators have noticed the gradual expansion of the harmless error to excuse many deviations from the law.

The error preservation requirement, harmless error, and their exceptions are the first line of defense in sustaining a conviction. Properly developed, they prevent the appellate court from reaching the merits of an issue. Careful attention to these requirements also enhances the credibility of other arguments in the brief.

LAW, FACT AND DISCRETION

Once an objection has been made properly, or that the requirements of plain error are likely to be satisfied, the appropriate standard of review must be established. Traditionally, defining an issue as one of law, or of fact, or within the discretion of the trial judge, determined the standard of review. Generally, questions of law are reviewed de novo and that standard provides the appellate court with the greatest ability to overturn the trial court. Questions of fact are subject to a review for the reasonableness of the result,[22] and are entitled to substantial deference. Facts decided by the jury, in practice, are given great deference because they are protected by the state and federal constitutions.[23] Facts found by the judge are evaluated under the clearly erroneous standard. Matters committed to the discretion of the court are reviewed for abuse of that discretion. This test is the most deferential to the trial court's judgment and provides the least authority to the appellate court to change the decision.

As with many legal categories, the concepts of fact, law, and discretion are easy to articulate but are clear only at the extremes. In practice, these categories merge into each other making the analysis more difficult as seen from the disagreements among commentators and courts on many issues. It is easy to classify the defendant's presence on a street corner at 2:00 a.m. as a fact, but the finding that he was loitering or acting suspiciously implicates legal considerations and standards and subtly moves the issue into a different category. Nonetheless, these categories are the starting point.

1. Questions Of Law

A de novo standard governs questions of law. The appellate court may reconsider any question of law and may reach a different conclusion than the trial judge. The decision of the lower court is entitled only to the deference generated by its inherent logic or persuasiveness. Appellate judges, acting in a panel, trained in the law in the same manner as the trial judge, and perhaps helped by their more contemplative position, are as capable as the trial judge in determining the law, and may reconsider any interpretation of the law made below.

Also, entitled to a de novo standard are mixed questions of law and fact.[24] Mixed questions are those "in which historical facts are admitted or established, the rule of law is undisputed, and the issue is whether the facts satisfy the statutory standard, or to put it another way whether the rule of law as applied to the established facts is or is not violated."[25] Whether a defendant knowingly, and voluntarily waived his right against self-incrimination is a mixed question of law and fact, as is whether counsel was constitutionally ineffective. Some courts separate the mixed question into its factual and legal components and apply the appropriate test to each. The historical facts of who, what, where and when are tested under the clearly erroneous standard, while legal issues are addressed de novo.

Although questions of law are reviewed de novo, the depth of that review depends upon the task before the appellate court. Careful analysis of the facts of the case, and the precedent on the particular issue may allow the advocate to argue for more or less review within the de novo standard. The most searching examination of the trial judge's decision of law, its rationale and supporting facts occurs when the court is asked to create or expand new precedent. For example, the Supreme Court's decision in *Crawford v. Washington*,[26] which overturned a quarter century of constitutional law on confrontation and hearsay, undoubtedly will generate many questions of law, and mixed questions of law and fact. Appellate courts will reach for these issues, and probe the alternatives, to resolve the many unanswered questions in the opinion. Interpretation of the case law and the construction of statutes may be probing, depending upon the issue and whether the facts fall into recurring and previously seen scenarios. Applying settled law to recurring fact patterns generally demands less scrutiny by the reviewing court when the decision is prima facie acceptable.

The advocate can shape the appellate court's depth of review by clearly stating the legal task before it. Is the court being asked to apply law to novel or unusual facts, or to interpret case law or a statute, or is it just the application of established law to the facts found below. The tone of the brief and the supporting facts can suggest that the issue falls well within precedent, and need not be examined in depth, or in appropriate cases, that the proper development of the law is at stake, requiring a careful analysis by the court.

2. Questions Of Fact

The label "fact" is given to different findings. The most basic are historical, empirical or primary facts—the who, what, where and when, issues. These are established by direct or circumstantial evidence, and without the application of any legal principle. Primary or historical facts are subject to a standard more deferential to the initial decision maker, often the jury in criminal cases. Guilt, the ultimate fact issue decided by the jury in a criminal case, is entitled to great deference. In reviewing the evidence in support of a jury verdict, the court draws all inferences from the facts, and all credibility determinations in favor of the government and asks only whether the jury could have found each element beyond a reasonable doubt.[27] Facts determined by the jury can only be overturned when there is no basis in the record for that finding.

In the federal system, facts decided by the judge in considering objections, deciding motions and other rulings, are measured by the "clearly erroneous" standard. "A finding is 'clearly erroneous' when, although there is evidence to support it, the reviewing court on the entire evidence is left with the definite and firm conviction that a mistake has been made."[28] This standard requires the reviewing court to find something more than substantial evidence, which is often defined as any evidence in the record that supports the decision, even if reasonable persons could reach another conclusion. They must find that the conclusion reached by the trial judge is not mistaken when viewed in the context of the entire record. This is something more than mere disagreement with the trial judge. Clearly erroneous means that the "court's findings are presumptively correct."[29] Another court conveyed this meaning in different, but quite effective language. "[T]he decision must strike us as more than just maybe or probably wrong; it must... strike us as wrong with the force of a five-week-old unrefrigerated dead fish."[30]

In analyzing the standard of review for facts, the lawyer must distinguish historical facts from those reached by the application of law to facts, which are mixed questions of law and fact. For example, whether a witness with particular knowledge, training and experience is an expert requires applying the legal standards of Fed. R. Evid. 702, to the known historical facts about the witness's background. The decision to admit or exclude that witness's testimony is a mixed question of law and fact and subject to a de novo review by the appellate courts. Appellate judges, however, often apply the more deferential factual standard of review to the purely historical facts of the witness's experience.

3. Questions Committed To The Discretion Of The Court

Many trial decisions, especially the management of the courtroom and conduct of the trial, are committed to the discretion and judgment of the trial judge. The exercise of discretion is the exercise of choice. In many situations there is no one correct answer, and many decisions are plausible and acceptable. The appellate court defers to the trial judge's choice simply because the decision falls within broad range of acceptable alternatives, and the judge, having sat in the courtroom, had access to more information about the parties, issues and trial than can be gleaned from the cold transcript. The abuse of discretion standard is applied to those issues.

Abuse of discretion generally favors the respondent whose interest is in preserving the result at the trial. Nevertheless, the discretion of the trial court, although broad, is not unlimited, unreviewable or unreversible. Issues are subject to varying degrees of deference. There are a few issues, which because of their inherent nature, or the infinite complexity of the considerations, will not be overturned except in truly unique cases. Many courtroom management issues fall into this category. Similarly, the appellate court may accept the judge's decision on a novel issue because there is no case law against which to measure an apparently reasonable decision.

Other issues, ostensibly committed to the discretion of the trial court, are subject to constraints by established precedent. The appellate court may have established a framework for analysis, a list of factors to be considered, a requirement to articulate the rationale, or perhaps a preferred outcome for all but the exceptional case. Here the trial court's discretion is more limited than implied by the abuse of discretion standard. The admission of prior crimes for impeachment, for example, not only must satisfy the Rule 609, but the balancing of probative value and prejudice. Case law identifies several factors to consider, including the nature of the impeaching crime, its recency or remoteness, similarity to the crime charge, nature and extent of records the importance of the defendant's testimony and the importance of credibility issues in the case.[31] Judges ignoring, misapplying or not referring to those standards, or not supporting the decision in the record, may be reversed.

The abuse standard is applied along a continuum and the careful lawyer will search the precedents with care to identify the factors that the appellate courts consider when reviewing discretionary decision. This standard provides the advocate ample opportunity to advance reasons for greater or lesser deference to a particular decision.

4. Advocacy And The Labels

The label of an issue as one of law, fact or discretion is not necessarily fixed and is subject to challenge and persuasive advocacy in many cases. Speaking of the law/fact distinction the Supreme Court ruefully noted that "we [do not] yet know of any other rule or principle that will unerringly distinguish a factual finding from a legal conclusion."[32]

The imprecision of the labels of fact, law and discretion presents the appellate advocate with a challenge and an opportunity. Analysis may reveal that a particular issue is subject to a more favorable standard. For example, what intuitively appears to be an issue committed to the discretion of the trial judge, such as the admission or exclusion or evidence, may be a mixed question of law and fact, subject to a de novo standard of review. Appellants' counsel are told to attempt to transmute discretionary questions into mixed questions of law and fact that are reviewed de novo.[33] The appellate prosecutor should anticipate this tactic, and be prepared to contest it, or meet the issue on appeal on the merits.

Even if an issue falls within one of the broad categories of fact, law and discretion, counsel have the opportunity to frame the issue toward the more favorable end of the spectrum. Historical facts are given more deference than those requiring a chain of inferences. Recurring questions of law often are applied by force of precedent rather than analysis. Even decisions committed to the discretion of the court, the most deferential standard, often rest upon the application of legal principles to facts found by the judge, and are limited, albeit loosely by case law.

Commentators suggest that the designation of an issue as one of law, or one of fact or committed to the judge's discretion is really a conclusion that a particular issue is more appropriately decided by either the trial judge, or the appellate court. Judge Posner wrote, "'Law' and 'fact' do not in legal discourse denote preexisting things; they express policy-grounded legal conclusions. We ought to ask what is gained and what is lost by appellate second-guessing of a federal district judge's determination."[34] De novo review, is justified because the appellate court is in the better position to make the final decision on an issue. Likewise, a holding that a matter is within the discretion of the trial judge, or committed to the fact finder, is one explained by the judge or jury's better vantage point when making that decision.

The advocate, faced with the task of persuading the appellate court to use a different standard, or at least view the issue at the more favorable end of the category, must examine the record, the issue and the case law carefully for supporting arguments. The primary argument for deferring to the trial court is the better perspective the judge has on the issue from being in the courtroom. Questions dependent upon assessing the credibility of witnesses, or reconciling conflicting testimony or documentary evidence, are better left to the trial judge in large part because a transcript cannot convey the nuances available to the trial judge making the decision.[35]

One appellate judge explained it this way:

> The trial judge saw and heard the plaintiff; saw his twitchings, what they were and what they were not, as did the jury. He saw or heard the other matters relied on by the appellant; he felt the "climate" of the trial. The trial judge found no fraud or misrepresentation.... The Court of Appeals should not and will not substitute its judgment for that of the trial court, nor reverse the law court's determination save for an abuse of discretion.[36]

A second argument for leaving matters with the trial court is that the decision making process is so multifaceted, and the weighing of the conflicting considerations so complex, that little is gained from having it reconsidered on appeal. Sentencing in criminal cases, prior to the creation of statutory Sentencing Guidelines, was an example of such an issue best left to the trial judge who made the initial decision. A contributing factor to this deference often is that the competing considerations do not clearly appear in the record. The novelty of an issue also suggests deference to the trial court, at least initially, simply because there may be no appropriate standards in the law, and sufficient experience has not been gained to abstract guiding principles.

The arguments for a de novo standard are also based on the appellate court's better perspective on certain issues. To the extent that an issue does not depend on credibility determinations, or the judgments of the person in the courtroom, but relies on essentially undisputed facts, argues for independent review and final decision by an appellate panel.

The appellate court's function is, in part, to guide and develop the law into a coherent and consistent structure. This obligation favors appellate review in two situations. First, some issues, regardless of their intuitive characterization, must be reviewed to accomplish this goal. One United States Supreme Court opinion expressed the concept:

> A finding of fact in some cases is inseparable from the principles through which it was deduced. At some point, the reasoning by which a fact is "found" crosses the line between application of those ordinary principles of logic and common experience which are ordinarily entrusted to the finder of fact into the real of a legal rule upon which the reviewing court must exercise its own independent judgment. Where the line is drawn varies according to the nature of the substantive law, the stakes—in terms of impact on future cases and future conduct—are too great to entrust them finally to the judgment of the trier of fact.[37]

The Supreme Court in *Ornealas v. United States*[38] held that a probable cause finding is reviewed as a mixed question of law and fact, in part because "the legal rules for probable cause and reasonable suspicion acquire content only through application. Independent review is therefore necessary if appellate courts are to maintain control of, and to clarify, the legal principles."[39]

A second reason for appellate review occurs when an area of the law has sufficiently matured to require appellate guidance. Many matters originally committed to the discretion of the trial judge over time, are transmuted into mixed questions of law and fact. At first, the appellate court defers to the trial judge because the issue is too new to predict its ramifications and the trial judge's decision is not obviously wrong. As more cases are appealed, the appellate court first develops general guidelines, and then more detailed framework for decision. Advocacy probably makes the difference in whether the appellate court considers the issue ripe for defining the limits of discretion.

CONCLUSION

Standards of review are the first point of conflict between the appellant and respondent. They define the depth of review and do influence the outcome of the appeal in many cases. A sound legal argument is an interplay of the facts found below, the substantive law, and the standards of review. As with the law and facts, standards of review provide another place for effective advocacy. While the standards of review generally follow the categories of law, fact, and matters of discretion, these labels are not monolithic. Facts, law and discretion are malleable concepts and categories, and the advocate should not accept them as given, and should search the record for facts and reasons that support a favorable standard, or a more favorable perspective, within that standard. The highest skill of the advocate is to take the inherently dry topic of the standard of review and give it life in the context of the case so it may play its essential and often decisive role.

ENDNOTES

[1] See Fed. R. App. P 28(a)(9)(B and (b)(5) which require the appellant and respondent to state the standard of review.

[2] On the general topic of standards of review see, George A. Somerville, *Standards of Appellate Review, Appellate Practice Manual* p. 16 (ABA Section on Litigation 1992); Ruggero J. Aldisert, *Winning on Appeal*, (Rev. 1st ed. NITA Practical Guide Series, 1996); Steven Alan Childress, *A Standards of Review Primer: Federal Civil Appeals*, 125 F.R.D. 310 (1995). For particular standards see, 157 A.L.R. Fed. 521 (harmless error); Maurice Rosenberg, *Appellate Review of Trial Court Discretion*, 79 F.R.D. 173 (1978).

[3] Michael R. Bosse, *Standards of Review: The Meaning of Words*, 49 Me. L. Rev. 367 (1997) (Maine).

[4] Almost every sentence could have been footnoted to the major works cited above. I have chosen not to do so in an effort to eschew prolixity and creeping law review citationism. This is not to underestimate or conceal my debt to the authors on whom I relied.

[5] Fed. R. Crim. P. 51; Fed. R. Evid. 103(a).

[6] Fed. R. Evid. 103(a)(2) (offer of proof).

[7] See e.g, *Parr v. Gaines*, 424 S.E.2d 515 (S.C. Ct. App. 1992).

[8] South Carolina does not have a plain error standard. See S.C.R.E. 104 (omitting plain error standard for evidence objections; *Dilliplanine v. Lehigh Valley Trust Co.*, 322 A.2d 114, 116-17 (Pa. 1974).

[9] See also Fed. R. Evid. 103(d).

[10] Johnson v. United States, 520 US 461, 467-68 (1993).

[11] *Olano v. United States*, 507 U.S. 725, 734-35 (1993).

[12] *Id.*

[13] *Supra* n. 10.

[14] For those who want to be diverted from writing the brief by seeking the official citation to the origin of the phrase, see, Linda E. Carter, *The Sporting Approach to Harmless Error in Criminal Cases: The Court's "No Harm, No Foul" Debacle in Neder v. United States*, 28 Am. J. Crim. Law 229, 230 n.3 (2001). (No, not that Linda Carter).

[15] *Chapman v. California*, 386 U.S. 18 (1967).

[16] *Rose v. Clark*, 478 U.S. 570 (1986).

[17] *Holloway v. Arkansas*, 435 U.S. 474, 488 (1978 (abridgment of the right to counsel); *Chapman v. California*, 386 U.S. 18 (1967 (impartial judge).

[18] "Any error, defect, irregularity, or variance that does not affect substantial rights must be disregarded. Fed. R. Crim. P. 52(a).

[19] "Error may not be predicated upon a ruling which admits or excludes evidence unless a substantial right of the party is affected." Fed. R. Evid. 103(a).

[20] *Kotteakos v. United States*, 328 U.S. 750, 764-65 (1946) reaffirmed in *O'Neal v. McAninch, 513, U.S. 432 (1995).*

[21] Christopher B. Mueller & Laird C. Kirkpatrick, Evidence § 7.1 at 23 (3rd ed. 2003).

[22] 2 Steven Alan Childress and Martha S. Davis, *Federal Standards of Review* § 7.05 at 7-26 (2nd ed. 1992).

[23] The Seventh Amendment provides: "no fact tried by a jury shall otherwise be re-examined in any Court of the United States, than according to the rules of the common law. Many states have comparable provisions. See e.g., S. C. Const. Art. I § 5 The

> [Supreme] Court shall have appellate jurisdiction only in cases of equity, and in such appeals they shall review the findings of fact as well as the law, exception cases where the facts are settled by a jury and the verdict not set aside."

[24] See generally, Evan Tsen Lee, "Principled Decision Making and the Proper Role of Federal Courts: The Mixed Question of Law Conflict." 64 S. Cal. L. Rev. 235 (1991).

[25] *Pullman-Standard v. Swint*, 456 U.S. 273, 289 n.19 (1982).

[26] 124 S.Ct. 1354 (2004).

[27] *Glasser v. United States*, 315 U.S. 60, 62 (1942).

[28] *United States v. United States Gypsum Co.*, 333 U.S. 364, 395 (1948).

[29] Charles Alan Wright & Arthur R. Miller, *Federal Practice and Procedure* § 2585 at 565 (2 ed. 1995).

[30] *Parts & Elec. Motors, Inc. v. Sterling Elec., Inc.*, 866 F.2d 228 (7th Cir. 1988).

[31] Meuller & Kirkpatrict § 631 at 497-500.

[32] *Pullman-Standard v. Swint*, 456 U.S. 273, 288 (1982).

[33] Michael E. Tigar and Jane B. Tigar, *Federal Appeals, Jurisdiction and Practice* § 5.07 at 287 (3rd ed. 1999).

[34] *Weidner v. Thietrt*, 866 F.2d 958, 961 (7th Cir. 1989).

[35] Ronald R. Hofer, *Standards of Review – Looking Beyond the Labels*, 74 Marq. L. Rev. 231, 242 (1991).

[36] *Atchison, Topeka & Santa Fe Ry. Co. v. Barnett*, 246 F.2d 846, 849 (9th Cir 1957) (citations omitted).

[37] *Bose v. Consumers Union of United States, Inc.*, 466 U.S. 485, 501 n.17 (1984).

[38] 116 S.Ct. 1657 (1996).

[39] *Id* at 1662.

NINE

PROTECTING THE RECORD FOR APPEAL:
Advice For The Trial Prosecutor

J. KIRK BROWN
NEBRASKA'S SOLICITOR GENERAL
LINCOLN, NEBRASKA

I always pass on good advice. It is the only thing to do with it. It is never of any use to oneself.

Oscar Wilde (1854—1900)

This chapter is dedicated to and directed at my trial prosecutor colleagues who may or may not represent the people on appeal. As trial attorneys we understand that there often exists a difference between what one *knows* to be true and what one can *prove* to be true. In appellate work there is a corresponding truism: A difference exists between what one *knows* happened at trial and what one can *prove* happened at trial. That difference hinges upon the nature of the record made at trial.

In this chapter we will discuss both the trial rules which impact the creation of an appeal-worthy record and an approach to trial which anticipates the creation of an appeal-worthy record.

ANTICIPATING THE APPEAL DURING TRIAL

As a trial prosecutor, your immediate focus has to be to seek a conviction, provided of course that is the just result. However, I suggest to you that trying a case without anticipating the likelihood of appellate review of the trial's result shortsighted. A victory at trial is of little value if that victory cannot be preserved on appeal. A loss at trial of a pretrial suppression motion, for example, remains a loss forever if it cannot be reversed on appeal. Our general goal on appeal is to do everything possible to preserve our victories and erase our losses through the process of appellate review. Our specific goal is to understand the role an appropriately preserved and presented trial record plays in reaching that goal.

Every case should be tried with the anticipation that the ruling and conviction rendered will be appealed. Regardless of the trial prosecutor's role in any subsequent appeal, it is important for a trial prosecutor to make every effort to have the trial record contain everything necessary to either (1) affirm a trial judge's ruling in your favor, or (2) discredit the trial judge's ruling against you before the appellate court. You will not know, in the course of trial, whether the trial will reach a satisfactory conclusion.

On appeal in criminal matters, the appellate prosecutor is the appellee (resxpondent) in almost all appeals.[1] Therefore, these comments focus upon how an appellee approaches an appellate record. The more the trial prosecutor understands about how their conviction will be defended on appeal, the more likely the trial record will be wholly capable of being successfully defended on appeal.

The role of appellee (respondent) is defensive. As an appellee, we have prevailed in the trial court and obtained a conviction. We now seek to preserve that victory through the course of appellate review. The role of counsel for the appellee is to know the strength of your case and determine the weaknesses of the appellant's case.

With respect to each claim of error, the appellee's first role is to assist the appellate court in discovering if the appellant's claim of error may even be appropriately considered on its merits. Often the condition of the appellate record answers that question and assists us in achieving our goal.

TRUTH IS FOUND IN COMPLETENESS

Furthermore, as representatives of the people, we appellate prosecutors have an additional and appropriate responsibility to see that justice is served by what we do throughout the litigation process. Justice is best achieved when the record made at trial and the record made available to an appellate court is as complete, as accurate and as detailed as possible.

In some jurisdictions, a tradition exists of conducting significant discussions between the trial court and trial counsel off the record. I strongly encourage you to do all within your power to have as much of your pretrial, trial and post-trial proceedings on the record.

On appeal, the people we represent obtain absolutely no benefit from these silences in the record. On the other hand, I regularly observe the defense bar fill such silences with inflammatory speculation which proves disturbing to the appellate courts and is impossible for the appellate prosecutor to rebut.

You will sometimes be surprised to discover that an appellant has asserted a claim of error on appeal and yet failed to order from the trial court those materials in the trial record which would allow evaluation of the claim of error asserted. It is incumbent upon a appellee to discover if such an oversight has occurred. The record ordered by an appellant may also contain inadvertent or intentional omissions essential to the appellate court's understanding of the correctness of the trial court's ruling in favor of the government. Therefore, the appellee must be aware of local roles permitting augmentation of the appellate record when deemed necessary to make the appellee's case. It is incumbent upon the trial prosecutor and appellate prosecutor, assuming they are not one and the same person, to communicate with one another to insure that the complete and relevant trial record gets before the appellate bench.

PRESERVING ERROR

Occasionally the appellate prosecutor is the appellant, for example when pursuing review of an adverse pretrial ruling on a defense suppression motion or when cross appealing. In that situation it is absolutely essential that the trial prosecutor create a record at trial which preserves any potential claims of error for appellate review. A failure to do so at the trial level will generally either (1) provide the appellate court a legitimate reason not to address that claim of error upon its merits, or (2) require that the claim of error be subject to an appellate standard of review which (a) the appellate court may or may not choose to employ and (b) which, if employed, is extremely difficult for an appellant to overcome—plain error.[2]

As a general proposition Rule 51, *Federal Rules of Criminal Procedure,* articulates trial counsel's obligations with respect to preserving a claim of error for appellate review. "(I)t is sufficient that a party, (1) at the time the ruling or order of the court is made or sought, (2) makes known to the court the action which the party desires the court to take or that party's objection to the action of the court and (3) the grounds therefore,...."

Rule 103, *Rules of Evidence for United States Courts and Magistrates,* defines the basic manner in which trial counsel must preserve for appellate review evidentiary rulings of the trial court. To do so trial counsel must: (1) make a timely objection or motion to strike upon the record; (2) state the specific ground of the objection, and (3) make an offer of proof regarding the evidence desired to be introduced if an objection to that evidence is sustained

Don't Just Object. Articulate Your Legal Theory On The Record

Although each step of this process of making a record is crucial, on appeal the most important step is often the articulation of the theory under which the objection is raised. Appellate courts are reluctant to overturn trial court rulings upon a theory which was not specifically articulated to and ruled upon by the trial court.[3] Therefore, to satisfy the requirements of Rule 103 trial counsel must both: anticipate, as best you can, the objections you will be making or opposing and articulate clearly and specifically upon the trial record the theory under which you assert or oppose that objection.

Trial judges vary greatly with respect to the amount and detail of analysis they share upon the record when ruling on objections. If the appellate court is to have a clear understanding of the question ruled on by the trial court, it is incumbent upon the trial prosecutor, whether making or responding to an objection, to place upon the record in some detail the nature of the question the trial court is being asked to rule.

Know When To Object

Pretrial and post-trial rulings by the trial court are governed by the same requirements for specificity and articulation. With pretrial and post-trial rulings, however, making a timely objection is often the more complex aspect of preserving an objection for appellate review. It is important to understand the point in time when your local rules require that objections be made to these types of rulings. For example, if the result of a pretrial hearing allows certain evidence to be offered at trial, must the trial prosecutor object a second time when such evidence is offered at trial or does the objection which prompted the pretrial hearing suffice to preserve that objection for appellate review? You need to know the answer to such questions in your jurisdiction.

Rule 12(f), *Federal Rules of Criminal Procedure,* provides with respect to pretrial pleadings and motions: "Failure by a party to raise defenses or objections or to make requests which must be made prior to trial… shall constitute waiver thereof…"

Jury Instructions

Rule 30, *Federal Rules of Criminal Procedure,* provides with respect to jury instructions: "No party may assign as error any portion of the charge or omission therefrom unless that party objects thereto before the jury retires to consider its verdict, stating distinctly the matter to which the party objects and the grounds of the objection."

CONCLUSION

The record you make at trial normally is the single most critical factor in any appeal. The more complete the trial record, the more specific your objections, the more articulate you are in expressing those objections and the theories which support them, the firmer a foundation for success on appeal the trial record becomes.

ENDNOTES

[1] See chapter 11 on State's appeals.

[2] Rule 52(b), *Federal Rules of Criminal Procedure.*

[3] "In general, preserving an issue is a matter of making a timely objection to the trial court and clearly stating the grounds for the objection, so that the trial court has an opportunity to prevent or correct the error in the first instance." *U.S. v. Thornberg,* 844 F.2d 573, 575 (8th Cir. 1988)

TEN

PROFESSIONAL RESPONSIBILITY ON APPEAL

BARBARA P. HERVEY
JUDGE, TEXAS COURT OF CRIMINAL APPEALS
AUSTIN, TEXAS

MICHAEL E. KEASLER
JUDGE, TEXAS COURT OF CRIMINAL APPEALS
AUSTIN, TEXAS

The qualities of a good Prosecutor are as elusive and as impossible to define as those which mark a gentleman. And those who need to be told would not understand it anyway. A sensitiveness to fair play and sportsmanship is perhaps the best protection against the abuse of power, and the citizen's safety lies in the prosecutor who tempers zeal with human kindness, who seeks truth and not victims, who serves the law and not factional purposes, and who approaches his task with humility.

Justice Robert H. Jackson, formerly Solicitor General of the United States.

We all know that allegations of "prosecutorial misconduct" are too often raised in criminal cases. Although many of these involved are leveled at trial prosecutors, an appellate prosecutor is also obliged to do the right thing. Additionally, as an appellate prosecutor, you will be faced with the responsibility of addressing these claims on appeal. The following scenarios present possible appellate dilemmas, with suggested solutions and citations to the American Bar Association Model Rules of Professional Conduct (hereafter RPC), which have been adopted by 42 states. Remember: the same ethical rules apply to appellate prosecutors as those for trial prosecutors and all lawyers alike.

The following is a series of eight situations which confront the appellate prosecutor along with some thoughts on ethical responses to them. While you may not run into the exact situations posed, it is likely that you will encounter something like them. At least, the following discussion will acquaint or re-acquaint you with essential ethical boundaries for your appellate practice.

1. Candor, Competence And The Pressing Workload

You are rushed for time on your brief and have three others on your desk needing immediate attention. You have read a million cases with similar issues and decide that you can skim the record. Consequently, your brief contains errors both of substance and of citations to the record. At oral argument, the court interrogates you about several of the factual misstatements in your brief.

What do you do?

Now is the time to 'fess up. It is likely the justices have read the record or at least have bench memoranda from attorneys highlighting your errors. You are only as good as your reputation, and your reputation will be attributed to other members of your office. As Albert Schweitzer said, "You do not live in a world all alone. Your brothers are here, too." If you misrepresent matters to the judges, they will remember and will have trouble believing you and your colleagues in the future.

That is not all. Because you were swamped for time, you did not add record references to your brief. You have also failed to *Shepardize* your cases to give subsequent history. You find time to supplement your brief and do so, but rely on unpublished cases.

Have you violated any ethical rules?

Yes. Not only are you required to be thorough, but you are required to know the existing law, statutes, court rules, codes, regulations and so on. Unpublished cases are not considered controlling cases in most jurisdictions, and the court justifiably expects valid references to the record. The court demands at least standard legal research and good legal reasoning. If you find yourself uncertain in a particular area of the law, asking for assistance from colleagues or additional self-study would be wise. Also, inexperience is no excuse for poor performance.

RPC 1.1 on Competence provides:

> A lawyer shall provide competent representation to a client. Competent representation requires the legal knowledge, skill, thoroughness and preparation reasonably necessary for the representation.

RPC 3.3 Candor toward the Tribunal states:

> (a) A lawyer shall not knowingly:
>> (1) make a false statement of fact or law to a tribunal or fail to correct a false statement of material fact or law previously made to the tribunal by the lawyer

2. Communication With The Bench—Your Best Friend

Your best friend and colleague in the prosecutor's office has just been elected to the trial bench. She has never been an appellate expert, and she does not care much for legal research. In the past, she has always relied on your research and legal reasoning. She wants to continue this arrangement, ex parte. She calls you constantly for advice during trial.

How do you respond?

A lawyer may communicate in writing to a judge, but only if the documents are simultaneously delivered to opposing counsel and the judge is informed of the delivery and the fact that counsel has not yet had an opportunity to respond. The applicable RPC is 3.5 Impartiality and Decorum of the Tribunal, which provides:

> A lawyer shall not:
> (a) Seek to influence a judge, juror, prospective juror, or other official by means prohibited by law;
> (b) communicate ex parte with such a person during the proceeding unless authorized to do so by court order;

(c) communicate with a juror or prospective juror after discharge of the jury if:

(1) the communication is prohibited by law or court order;

(2) the juror has made known to the lawyer a desire not to communicate; or

(3) the communication involves misrepresentation, coercion, duress or harassment; or

(d) engage in conduct intended to disrupt a tribunal.

Note that the prohibition against ex parte communications is equally restrictive when the judge is the party initiating the ex parte communication.

We suggest three ways to handle the judge:

a. Refuse to participate; request the presence of opposing counsel.

b. Inform opposing counsel of the judge's request and instructions.

c. Because the judge is your friend, it would be a good idea to explain that while your friendship is important, it is not proper for either of you to continue the exchange of legal knowledge as you did in the past.

Assume that you selected suggestions either a. or b. and c. above and that your best friend, the trial judge, just finished a high profile case involving a local celebrity. The prosecution and the defense agree that the judge's sentence was unduly harsh. The parties agree that the defendant should either receive a new trial or shock probation. You agree and believe that the judge would be better off if she showed leniency. The judge will listen to you.

Should you approach her?

Ex parte communications are wrong even if your motives are laudable. Perhaps, the defense should file its motion for new trial and the state can inform the court that it has no objections.

When can you talk to a judge about a case?

Upon final disposition. Of course, you can always approach the judge if you and opposing counsel do so together.

3. You Discover A New Case On All Fours

A few days before oral argument, you discover a case from another jurisdiction that strongly supports your position on appeal. You would like to tell the court of appeals about it in oral argument. Then, suppose it strongly supports the appellant's position.

Would it be appropriate to inform the court during oral argument?
If it supports the appellant's position, do you have to disclose it?
What are the alternatives?

You can tell the court about the case no matter which side it supports. If it is controlling authority supporting the appellant's position, you are obligated to disclose it. RPC 3.3 Candor Toward the Tribunal states:

(a) A lawyer shall not knowingly:

(2) fail to disclose to the tribunal legal authority in the controlling jurisdiction known to the lawyer to be directly adverse to the position of the client and not disclosed by opposing counsel.

Disclosure also includes statutes. Disclosure is required even if you feel your case can be factually distinguished. It has also been held that there is an implied duty to learn of adverse authority. Know what your court considers "controlling." Different interpretations exist as to what is meant by "controlling." For example, some decisions suggest that it means written by a court superior to the one hearing the case.

Here, the case authority is from another jurisdiction, and some appellate courts disavow cases from other jurisdictions completely, and RPC 3.3 specifically states that the lawyer must disclose legal authority "in the controlling jurisdiction." Unless the appellate court clearly does not accept authority from another jurisdiction, it would be wise to disclose the other jurisdictions case authority under circumstances where no appellate court has addressed the legal issue before the court and the majority of other jurisdictions have adopted the appellant's position.

The best practice is to provide copies of the case to both appellant's counsel and the court before argument. If you do not have time to have the cases copied for the bench and opposing counsel before the argument, cite the case and offer to supplement with a letter brief.

Now, assume that the adverse decision you found is from the federal court of appeals in your district. In its opinion the court invalidates your position in a case indistinguishable from your own. Must you cite the opinion as adverse, controlling authority?

Yes, again, if your court considers case law from the federal courts controlling.

4. New Adverse Decision—Dodge Bullet By Waiving Argument?

You have just completed the monster brief of all time. Just hours before your oral argument before the intermediate appellate court on what you thought was an absolute winner, the high court hands down an opinion that appears to blow you out of the water.

What do you do?

While waiving argument may seem tempting, RPC 3.3 discussed in situation number 3 above obligates you to inform the court of this new wrinkle in your case. If you do not have time to make copies of this case, at least inform the court of the apparently controlling decision, offering to supplement your brief. Supplement your brief if you are able to distinguish your case from the new decision.

5. Doing Justice And Actual Innocence

You are an appellate prosecutor, who does not carry a trial load of cases. Several years before our employment with the prosecutor's office, a very high-profile case was tried, and the defendant was given a life sentence. The defendant has mailed you a series of documents that indicate he is actually innocent.

What do you do?

The answer is easy because you, like all prosecutors, are a minister of justice whose goal it is to seek justice. This duty was pronounced by the United States Supreme Court in *Berger v. United States,* 295 U.S. 78, 88 (1935):

> [The prosecutor] is the representative not of an ordinary party to a controversy, but of a sovereignty whose obligation to govern impartially is as compelling as its obligation to govern at all; and whose interest, therefore, in a criminal prosecution is not that it shall win a case, but that justice shall be done. As such, he is in a peculiar and very definite sense the servant of the law, and the twofold aim of which is that guilt shall not escape or innocence suffer. He may prosecute with earnestness and vigor indeed, one should do so. But, while he may strike hard blows, he is not at liberty to strike foul ones. It is as much his duty to refrain from improper methods calculated to produce a wrongful conviction as it is to use every legitimate means to bring about a just one.

This situation presupposes that the defendant is actually innocent. Actual innocence is not a new concept, but it has become a national criminal justice issue. Because no one who participates in the system wants innocent people to be wrongly incarcerated, a united effort to investigate these claims and give relief in the meritorious ones is imperative. Many national organizations have worked on actual innocence claims. Some states have projects to handle these matters. Familiarizing yourselves with their methods of handling these claims is a good starting point in your decision to get involved with the process. Actual innocence covers more than DNA requests and includes such matters as recantations in sexual abuse cases and recantations of sole eyewitnesses.

Suggested methods of handling such claims include:

a. Screen the claims. Obviously, not every challenge will have merit. How do you define "actual innocence?" Does the term mean: "I was there, but someone else committed the crime"? Or, "I committed the crime, but I have a really good excuse"? Or does it simply mean, "I did not do it"?

b. For those claims that make it past your initial screening, have the matter investigated. Assign an investigator, if possible. The record and the appellate court opinions are very helpful at this point. Read your jurisdiction's case law on actual innocence.

c. Is there a request for DNA testing? Has this testing ever been performed? Conduct testing where necessary.

d. Have a plan to take these cases into court for the proper disposition.

6. You Learn Of Wrong-Doing

You are the appellate prosecutor, and during your initial preparation for appeal, you hear a rumor suggesting that the trial prosecutor convinced the trial judge to back-date an order crucial to your case. You are able to verify the wrong-doing.

What action do you take and against whom?

In a situation such as this knowing that another has committed a violation of the Rules of Professional Conduct, we all have a duty pursuant to RPC 8.3, Reporting Professional Misconduct, to report it to appropriate authorities. This applies to judicial misconduct as well. RPC 8.4, Misconduct, prohibits a lawyer from engaging in conduct that is prejudicial to the administration of justice, and further prohibits a lawyer from knowingly assisting a judge in conduct that violates the rules of judicial conduct.

Again, assuming that the back-dated order is crucial to your appellate argument, does an ethical rule prohibit you from advancing that argument?

RPC 3.1 Meritorious Claims and Contentions states:

> A lawyer shall not bring or defend a proceeding, or assert or controvert an issue therein, unless there is a basis in law and fact for doing so that is not frivolous, which includes a good faith argument for an extension, modification or reversal of existing law...

Also see RPC 3.3 Candor toward the Tribunal which would obligate you to inform the court of the falsehood.

7. You Really Want To Talk To The Reporter

One of your best friends is a prominent reporter with the local newspaper. The Court of Appeals has just handed down a controversial opinion in your case. You lost, and you are angry. The reporter calls you to comment and gives you a rendition of the opinion that is totally incorrect, factually and legally. The case is pending further appeal.

Can you talk to the press?

What do you tell him?

You can discuss some limited things if the case is ongoing. Those things are set out in RPC 3.6, which provides:

(a) A lawyer who is participating or has participated in the investigation or litigation of a matter shall not make an extrajudicial statement that the lawyer knows or reasonably should know will be disseminated by means of public communication and will have a substantial likelihood of materially prejudicing an adjudicative proceeding in the matter.

(b) Notwithstanding paragraph (a), a lawyer may state:

(1) the claim, offense or defense involved and, except when prohibited by law, the identity of the persons involved;

(2) information contained in a public record;

(3) that an investigation of a matter is in progress;

(4) the scheduling or result of any step in the litigation;

(5) a request for assistance in obtaining evidence and information necessary thereto;

(6) a warning of danger concerning the behavior of a person involved, when there is reason to believe that there exists the likelihood of substantial harm to an individual or to the public interest; and

(7) in a criminal case, in addition to subparagraphs (1) through (6):

(i) the identity, residence, occupation and family status of the accused;

>> (ii) if the accused has not been apprehended, information necessary to aid in the apprehension of that person;
>>
>> (iii) the fact, time and place of arrest; and
>>
>> (iv) the identity of investigating and arresting officers or agencies and the length of the investigation.
>
> (c) Notwithstanding paragraph (a), a lawyer may make a statement that a reasonable lawyer would believe is required to protect a client from the substantial undue prejudicial effect of recent publicity not initiated by the lawyer or the lawyer's client. A statement made pursuant to this paragraph shall be limited to such information as is necessary to mitigate the recent adverse publicity.
>
> (d) No lawyer associated in a firm or government agency with a lawyer subject to paragraph (a) shall make a statement prohibited by paragraph (a).

But, you should not give personal opinions or forecasts of the future outcome of an opinion as to the justness of the cause, the credibility of witnesses, or the guilt of the accused and so on while the case is pending. See RPC 3.4, Fairness to Opposing Counsel, which specifically restricts such statements during trial.

8. You Are Thinking About Criticizing The Appellate Judges

You are about to attend a major continuing legal education conference where several appellate judges will either speak or be in attendance. You are asked to deliver a speech on recent decisions.

Is there an appropriate level of criticism that can be incorporated into your presentation?

There are some practical considerations here, beyond the general concept of respect for the judiciary. Common sense would dictate that heavy criticism of judges scrutinizing your work is not a good idea. Also, although it is perfectly permissible to disagree with an opinion of the court, personal attacks are not proper, and one can always find a way to disagree respectfully. This concept carries over to brief writing.

Remember, the court can strike a brief or other legal document it finds too offensive. The court may find your writings to be offensive to the court or to opposing counsel. Further, RPC 8.2 forbids false statements (knowingly or with reckless disregard) about a judge's qualifications or integrity.

ELEVEN

HOW APPEALING IS YOUR CASE?
Eight Considerations That May Influence A Decision To Appeal

HILARY L. BRUNELL
EXECUTIVE ASSISTANT PROSECUTOR
ESSEX COUNTY PROSECUTOR'S OFFICE
NEWARK, NEW JERSEY

(I)t is ordinarily the defendant, rather than the State, who initiates the appellate process, seeking not to fend off the efforts of the State's prosecutor but rather to overturn a finding of guilt made by a judge or a jury below.

Ross v. Moffitt, 417 U.S. 600, 610, 94 S.Ct. 2437, 41 L.Ed.2d 341 (1974)

When the United States Supreme Court wrote its decision in *Ross v. Moffitt*, it likened the appellate process to a battleground in which defense counsel serves as a "sword to upset a prior determination of guilt."[1] Although the call to appellate arms is ordinarily issued by the defense, it need not be. In every state, prosecutors can, if they choose, issue their own strike against the defendant's assault on justice.

The appellate prosecutor's weapons have different names in different states—interlocutory appeals, petitions, writs, emergent appeals—but all fifty states afford the prosecutor the right to appeal in one form or another. Some states allow the prosecutor to cross appeal a legal ruling following conviction;[2] others allow an appeal from an evidentiary ruling issue during trial.[3] Still other states allow the prosecutor to seek an advisory opinion on a reserved question of law[4] or on a certified question following the filing of a bill of exception.[5] Each time the appellate prosecutor seeks review from a suppression ruling, from a pretrial dismissal of an indictment, from an intermediate appellate ruling, or from a federal district court decision in a habeas case, the appellate prosecutor is wielding a powerful weapon.

Deciding when to use that weapon can be critical. A win in an appellate court can favorably affect any number of cases; a loss can be equally far reaching. The trick, of course, is to tell the winners from the losers. Only judgment and experience can help us determine whether a case has what it takes to justify an appeal. This chapter offers eight guidelines, in the form of questions, to help you in evaluating whether to appeal a case. A number of factual situations are offered to illustrate the application of these guidelines.

1. Is Your Case An Important One?

No government attorney's office has unlimited resources to devote to pursuing appeals. Appellate attorneys must, therefore, triage their cases. In many offices appellate resources are more likely to be devoted to high profile cases or cases involving serious crimes.

Assume the question to decide is whether to appeal the trial court's ruling suppressing a confession in a murder case. Because your case involves a murder, it is, by definition, a serious case—the kind to which the office will devote its resources.

2. Is There A Serious Injustice Which Must Be Corrected?

This type of question can be one of the most difficult to answer, depending on the nature of the appeal under consideration. When a trial ruling is involved, there may be a clash of opinions and considerations.

Again, assume that your case involves the suppression of a confession, a ruling which could have a potentially devastating impact on the State's case. However, the confession is not the only compelling piece of evidence. The defendant has a motive for the murder, and eyewitness testimony and firearms comparison evidence tie the defendant to the murder.

Despite the additional evidence, it might be argued that the State should never be forced to go to trial with less than all of its evidence. It might also be argued that the State has nothing to lose by appealing the suppression ruling. Both arguments are valid and warrant serious consideration. However, if an appeal delays the trial for a substantial period of time, the appeal might nevertheless be inadvisable. Delays compromise the integrity of the State's evidence, they are painful for victims and family members, they cause hardships to witnesses, and they can be costly to the State which must release its witnesses and attempt to reassemble them for a later trial date. All of these considerations must weigh in the balance.

In your case, the importance of the confession and the fact that none of the remaining evidence is foolproof may lead you to conclude that a serious injustice may occur unless an appeal is taken.

3. Does Your Case Have An Appealing Issue?

Some types of trial court rulings make poor candidates for appeal. For example, a trial court's decision that the probative value of evidence is outweighed by its unfair prejudice is a decision not likely to be overruled on appeal. Rulings that depend on the credibility assessments are virtually immune from appeal; decisions that depend on purely legal determinations are far better candidates for appeal.

An issue may have an importance beyond the individual case. New case law or statutes might have an impact on your office and require appellate review. Even a relatively minor case may become important if it presents an opportunity to litigate an important question that is not likely to re-appear in another case. Novel questions are especially good candidates for discretionary appeals because appellate courts, like you, are looking for the opportunity to make law.

In some states, the import of the issue on appeal presents a jurisdictional question. In those states, the appeal cannot be heard, even if a novel question is involved, unless it is demonstrated that the appellate issue is of great public importance[6] or would be in the interest of justice.[7] In your jurisdiction, the confession issue discussed above raises an important and substantial question. The confession was obtained from the defendant through a ruse—the defendant was shown a phony statement allegedly authored by a codefendant. Your intermediate appellate court recently decided *State v. Sonner,* holding that due process requires the suppression of a confession based on evidence fabricated by the police. Your appellate colleagues have been watching for the proper case to litigate the limits of the *Sonner* ruling.

The question you must decide is whether your case is the one for which you and your colleagues have been waiting or whether it might, instead, invite a further extension of *Sonner* The answer to your dilemma lies in research and an analysis of the facts. These issues are discussed under the following standards.

4. Will Appellate Courts Be Receptive To Your Case?

Research your issue enough to know whether you are embarking on friendly territory. Are there other appellate decisions on the same or related topics which indicate that the court is receptive to the type of argument you will be making?

Your research on the confession fact pattern reveals that prior to *State v. Sonner,* it was understood in your jurisdiction that voluntary confessions induced by deceptions were admissible. However, you also learn that the seminal case on this issue was decided in 1988 by an intermediate appellate court and the issue was not addressed again until the *Sonner* case. The state Supreme Court has not addressed the issue of a fabricated confession, but it recently held that a murder confession given by a suspect who voluntarily appears at police headquarters for questioning is inadmissible if the police fail to advise the suspect that they have a warrant for his arrest on the murder.

The fact that *Sonner* seemingly contradicts long standing precedent and the fact that the highest court in your jurisdiction has never addressed this issue gives the case a lot of appeal. However, you must decide if your case is sufficiently distinguishable from the *Sonner* rationale and the recent state Supreme Court case to litigate the issue.

5. Are Your Facts Sympathetic?

Law and research aside, the appeal of your case will be affected greatly by the sympathy factor. A case with a sympathetic victim and/or an unsympathetic defendant, for example, is an appealing case.

Again, assume that your case involves a phony statement allegedly given by an accomplice. You also learn that the statement details the defendant's involvement in a kidnap and murder of a young woman who was last seen with her child. The body of the woman has been found. The child's body has not been recovered and it is not known if the child is alive. Before the defendant is shown the phony statement, his demeanor is cool and self-assured. He agrees to waive his rights. He professes his innocence, and then he tries to trick his interrogators with false clues about the child's whereabouts. Upon reading the phony confession, the defendant begins to sweat profusely and tremble. Before he is finished reading, the defendant admits to be being an accomplice, but he assigns the role of principal to the codefendant.

It is clear from these facts that the defendant was willing to waive his rights and give a statement, albeit a false one, prior to the confrontation with the phony confession and that he was willing to employ a subterfuge of his own. Will these facts make the police tactics more palatable to the appellate court? The facts also suggest an urgent need to find information about a missing child. How much of an impact will this consideration have on the appellate court's review of your case?

6. What Is The State Of The Trial Record?

To complicate matters, in some jurisdictions interlocutory or emergent appeals can be filed from trial rulings without the full transcript of the proceedings. These decisions make poor candidates for appeal because they are generally rushed and are dependent on what is inevitably an imperfect recollection of the record.

Other questions concerning the viability of such an appeal may become apparent as you review the record. You are considering whether to file an appeal from a trial court ruling suppressing a brick of heroin that was seized from the defendant's automobile during a valid traffic stop. The heroin was found on the floor of the passenger seat of the car. The arresting officer testified that the defendant "appeared upset" when stopped by the police and "glanced nervously in the direction of the floor." The suppression record was based on stipulated facts, and it is otherwise barren as to of any other reason for the search. You feel that the question of reasonable suspicion is a close one in your jurisdiction, but the case involves the seizure of a considerable amount of drugs. Do you appeal despite the paucity of the record?

Now assume that you have won the suppression motion at the trial level and, upon reviewing the police reports which were marked as evidence at the motion, it is apparent that the drugs were in plain view at the time of their seizure. However, this was not offered as a basis for the search. Do you raise this issue on appeal? You consider *Dandridge v. Williams,* 397 U.S. 491, 475 n.6 (1970) holding that the prevailing party may assert any ground on appeal in support of his judgment below, whether or not that ground was relied upon or even considered by the trial court.

7. Is The Appellate Opinion Published?

While much of the foregoing discussion focused on pretrial rulings, the question of whether to appeal arises in other settings as well. Assume you have lost an appeal in an intermediate court on a jury selection issue.[8] The trial prosecutor excused a Caucasian male, a missionary of unknown affiliation, and an African-American male whose attire and name suggested that he was a Muslim and was devout in his faith. The trial prosecutor explained that he excused both of these individuals for the same reason, namely because of his belief "that people who tend to be demonstrative about their religions tend to favor defendants to a greater extent than do persons who are, shall we say, not as religious." The peremptory challenges are permitted by the trial court but on appeal, an intermediate court, in a divided opinion, reverses. Under the law of your jurisdiction, you have the right to review by the state Supreme Court. Should you seek further review?

One consideration is whether the appellate court's opinion is published. If it is, there is probably little to lose by pursing the case to the next level. Because a written adverse decision already exists, you risk little by inviting another court to write on the issue.

If the opinion is unpublished, you may wish to consider whether the high court in your state has staked out a position on peremptory challenges to constitutionally protected groups. Your research reveals that when it comes to peremptory challenges, the court invariably finds that the state constitution provides greater protections than its federal counterpart. You interpret this as a signal that the court will not be favorably disposed to race or religion based challenges. If you can make a convincing argument that the challenge in this case was not based on impermissible considerations, should you appeal?

8. Is A Loss Acceptable?

Even in the case of the suppressed confession, there may be policy questions that weigh heavily in the balance. An appeal of a trial ruling suppressing a confession obtained through questionable interrogation tactics, for example, can permanently mark the legal landscape in a way that is decidedly unfavorable to your cause.

Assume that in a public safety exception case, the trial court finds a valid exception to *Miranda,* but an intermediate court, in an unpublished opinion, reverses. You are concerned that the intermediate appellate courts in your state have never sustained a public safety exception to *Miranda* and that the high court in your state has not yet addressed the question. Is this the right case to raise the issue? While admission of the evidence about locating the gun would virtually assure a conviction, the robbery victim is available as a witness and will identify the juvenile. How does this information influence your decision?

In some cases the motivating force behind the appeal is a courthouse issue—an issue that is unique to your office and which compels an institutional response. For example, judges in your courthouse uniformly misread a particular rule of evidence—or a single judge repeatedly issues unfair rulings.

If your goal is to communicate institutional displeasure with the quality of rulings from a particular member of the bench, think long and hard before you appeal. While your office may be frustrated with a particular judge, consider the consequences of losing. If you lose the appeal, the only message you may succeed in communicating is that the judge's rulings have been endorsed by the appellate bench. This surely will do little to reform the errant judge.

Serious reflection is also required when you are being pressured to launch a losing appeal to vindicate a principle or because you "owe it to the victim's family." Your credibility with the appellate bench is a valuable commodity which should not be squandered.

Consider one last fact situation to illustrate a final point. Again, assume the suppression of a confession in a murder case. This time, however, the confession is given to a deacon of a Baptist church who is also a state trooper. The defendant, who is not a member of the congregation, is brought to the church to consult with a priest. The priest calls in the trooper/deacon and leaves the room. The defendant then indicates to the deacon that he wants to turn himself in to the police and gives a full confession. According to the *Baptist Deacon,* a manual published by the church which was made part of the record at the suppression motion, a deacon has spiritual as well as ministerial duties. The trial judge suppressed the confession, finding that the trooper was functioning as a clergyman and, therefore, the confession was protected by the priest-penitent privilege.

There are many issues to consider in deciding whether to appeal. Did the deacon identify himself as a trooper? (He did). Did he give the defendant *Miranda* warnings? (No). Did he frisk the defendant before speaking to him? (Yes). Can the trial proceed without the confession? (Yes). Another consideration is immediately apparent to you: although the question of whether a trooper/deacon is a clergyman is a novel and interesting question, it is one that is not likely to arise with any regularity. In fact, the very novelty of the question convinces you that no matter what the outcome of your appeal, this is not a case that will have a significant impact on law enforcement. You might, therefore, decide that this is truly the type of case in which you have nothing to lose by appealing.

One final note of caution: unless you are convinced that your appeal will have no consequences beyond your own case, you should not appeal without considering the impact of your loss on other prosecutions. Even if you don't mind losing, the rest of us might.

ENDNOTES

[1] *Ross v. Moffitt*, 417 U.S. 600, 610-611, 94 S.Ct. 2437, 41 L.Ed.2d 341 (1974).

[2] Texas Code of Criminal Procedure, Article 44.01(c).

[3] New Jersey Court Rule 2:9-8

[4] See e.g., Kansas Statutes § 22-3602(b)(3); Indiana Code § 35-38-4-2(4).

[5] Wyoming Statutes § 7-12-104(b) (1987)

[6] *See,* e.g., Florida Rules of Appellate Procedure 9.160(f)(1), which provides the District Court of Appeal with jurisdiction to consider a state's appeal from a non-final order of the county court if the question is certified to be of "great public importance."

[7] Under Utah Code § 77-18a-1(2)(e) (1999), the State may appeal a pretrial order suppressing evidence if the appellate court decides the appeal would be in the interest of justice.

[8] *Batson v. Kentucky*, 476 U.S. 79, 106 S.Ct. 1712, 90 L.Ed.2d 69 (1986).

TWELVE

SUCCESSFUL APPELLATE ORAL ADVOCACY

TIMOTHY A. BAUGHMAN
CHIEF OF RESEARCH, TRAINING, AND APPEALS
WAYNE COUNTY APPELLATE PROSECUTOR'S OFFICE
DETROIT, MICHIGAN

The best appellate lawyers will know about important milestones across the legal spectrum. They will keep up with new Supreme Court and . . . Circuit Court decisions . . . Appellate advocacy is, in essence, a business for legal intellectuals.

> Hon. Laurence Silberman, *Judge of the United States Court of Appeals for the District of Columbia Circuit, ABA Journal, "Litigation, Spring," 1994*

"Successful Appellate Oral Advocacy" is a daunting subject, at least if one wishes to go beyond the commonplace. This is not to say that the commonplace is unimportant, for indeed it is critical—thorough preparation, answering questions from the bench when asked rather than putting off the questioner, and the like, are essential to effective appellate oral advocacy. But these, one hopes, are emphasized in first year law school moot court classes. The remarks and suggestions that follow, gleaned from observation of oral advocacy during 30 years of appellate practice, are directed to both the appellate prosecutor who is an appellate specialist and to the generalist who handles the occasional appeal.

By way of preface, one should bear in mind that it is a fact of nature that some people simply are better speakers than others; some have a gift for oratory, a presence, as it were, which is advantageous in appellate argument. Most of us do not have this ability. But this does not mean we cannot deliver effective appellate arguments. As Abraham Lincoln admonished in some "Notes on the Practice of Law" in 1850, "if anyone, upon his rare powers of speaking, shall claim exemption from the drudgery of the law, his case is a failure in advance."[1] Those of us without talent for oratory can certainly be effective oral advocates; those who are gifted speakers cannot get by on their gift alone.

WHEN TO ARGUE—THE SMALL OR ROUTINE CASE

Not all cases involve engaging facts or complicated issues. Given that most jurisdictions have some form of automatic review of convictions gained by trial, and given a natural reluctance on the part of many defense counsel to file *Anders* motions to withdraw, a great many defendant's briefs are filed that are either frivolous or routine. And, in some jurisdictions, oral argument is not automatic, but determined by the court, with some courts more jealous of their time than others. But, where oral argument is routinely permitted, should the prosecutor argue all cases?

Practical considerations inform the inquiry—how busy is the appellate prosecutor, and how far away is the court? If time is better spent working on briefs or preparing arguments in more complex cases, than in arguing a routine case, then the prosecutor must allocate and employ the resources accordingly. This is particularly so if hundreds of miles must be traveled to the court. But where practical considerations do not control, the prosecutor should neither argue all cases, including the frivolous or routine, nor forego argument in all routine cases. There is a place for oral argument, at least on occasion, in the routine case (though likely none for argument in a frivolous case). Arguing the routine case on occasion is helpful especially to the prosecutor new to appellate work. It is helpful when the first oral argument a prosecutor makes is not one in a highly complex and important case or in one of first impression. Obtaining some level of comfort through experience is important, and it is advisable to gain some of that experience by arguing a number of routine cases. And, so long as the brief is well done, to give the judges the opportunity to put name and face together is a positive thing for the appellate advocate.

These oral arguments, however, are not of the sort that is given in the complex case or the case of first impression—what might be termed the "full blown" argument. In these routine cases the appellate prosecutor should be prepared to make a few points, bring the court up to date on any new developments in the law, and answer questions. The argument may be very short, as little as 3–5 minutes, but the judges are able to link the name and face, and the advocate establishes that the court's time will not be wasted by using the entire time allotted for argument when that is not necessary. In short, argument in the routine case, when possible, though it should not always be done, may be done sufficiently to establish the advocate as reliable, trustworthy and considerate of the court's time. But, though the full-blown argument of the type described below is not made, the prosecutor must nonetheless enter the courtroom prepared, for the judges may have questions even in the routine case, and the appellate prosecutor who is not prepared to answer them harms rather than enhances his or her reputation.

THE FULL BLOWN ARGUMENT

Open And Candid

> Always do right. This will gratify some people, and astonish the rest.
>
> *Mark Twain, February 16, 1901, speech*

Twain's suggestion, of course, extends to all areas of practice and encompasses the other suggestions. What is urged here is for the appellate prosecutor, and indeed, as public prosecutor in all situations, to always tell the truth: don't misstate it, don't hide it, don't shade it, don't bend it, don't distort it. Just tell it. This is not only good and right, it is effective. It has been said that "facts that are not frankly faced have a habit of stabbing us in the back,"[2] and this is undoubtedly true in appellate argument. The judges will know, sooner or later, that an advocate failed to disclose an important fact or case or misstated a fact or the law, and the advocate's cause will have been harmed, as well as the advocate's reputation, which can harm future cases; this is especially true for the prosecutor, who must always be an advocate for justice. If an appellate prosecutor can develop a reputation among the appellate bench for candor and honesty—that a statement made during argument regarding the facts or the law can be trusted—this goes a long way toward rendering his or her oral advocacy effective. Moreover, oral argument is the prosecutor's last chance not only to explain the strengths of the argument, but to deal with what might be perceived by the judges as its weaknesses, to explain why a damaging fact is not controlling, or, when properly viewed, not damaging at all. It is also an occasion to explain why a detrimental case is distinguishable, or, where not distinguishable, simply wrong. One cannot be a successful appellate advocate—cannot persuade the disinterested judges to the rightness of the position taken—except by dealing in candor and in truth with the facts and with the law. A prosecutor has no interest in doing otherwise.

Engaging The Bench

> The acme of judicial distinction is to look a lawyer straight in the eyes for two hours and not hear a damn word he says.
>
> *Chief Justice John Marshall*[3]

One of the most disconcerting things that can happen to a lawyer during oral argument is to notice that the judges before whom the argument is made have are either not paying attention to the argument, or appear baffled by it. Sometimes there is nothing the oral advocate can do to remedy this situation, and there is nothing that could have been done to prevent it. On many occasions, however, if the judges are uninterested or uncomprehending, it is because the argument is dull or incomprehensible, or both.

Make no mistake about it, engaging the judges is what the oral argument is all about. The prosecutor who approaches argument with the hope that the prepared argument can be delivered without untidy interruptions from the judges to interrupt the flow of the meticulously well thought out presentation errs grievously. The only thing worse than approaching argument in this manner is succeeding in it. The prosecutor should so structure the argument as to grab the attention of the judges from the outset, and almost to demand that questions be asked. Just as seminars on trial advocacy teach the importance of development of a theme in closing argument to juries, development of a theme, with an attention arresting opening line or statement, where possible, should be the goal of the prosecutor in appellate oral advocacy. This sort of theme is different from that developed for jury argument, as the focus is on legal issues, but still one can develop a theme by asking, in planning the argument, "what is this case—this issue—about?" How does it fit in the framework of the law of the particular field involved?

A brief example. In *Michigan v Summers*[4] the precise legal issue was whether the police when executing a search warrant were justified in detaining people found on the premises until the warrant was executed. The theme of the oral argument—what the case was perceived to be about—was the need for the police when executing a search warrant to be able to make a "full and safe" execution of the warrant; that is, to be able to find that which the warrant commanded them to search for and seize, while protecting themselves during the process. Using this theme was a great help not only in engaging the Court[5] but also establishing a framework within which the Court's questions could more readily be answered.

Discernment of an appropriate theme is only possible through preparation and diligence. The appellate prosecutor must understand his or the case, and it is helpful to seek the views of others in the office. In the complex case or case of first impression, particularly when arguing in the state's highest court (or perhaps the United States Supreme Court!), preparation includes practice, and practicing the argument before one's peers, and maybe also including attorneys from outside the office and academics, will help to refine the argument, identify a theme, and most importantly, anticipate questions that will be asked from the bench.

Answering Questions From The Bench

It's broccoli, dear.
I say it's spinach, and I say the hell with it.

E.B. White, cartoon caption

Just as there is room for the well-turned phrase in appellate writing, there is also room in oral argument for the elegant presentation. But though the development of a theme around which to construct the argument is to be encouraged, along with an opening line or statement which serves to compel the judges to sit up and take notice, this does not mean that it is appropriate or effective for the prosecutor to try to make the case into something it is not. Interesting and engaging does not mean hyperbolic and overblown. If the case does not have far reaching practical consequences, do not say it does. If it will affect few other cases, admit it. If no novel issue of law is presented, do not try to invent one. The judges will not appreciate it; they'll know it's "really spinach."

Nothing in life is so exhilarating as to be shot at without result.

Winston Churchill, The Malakand Field Force

If the argument should be so constructed as to command the attention of the judges and to foster the asking of questions, then the heart of effective oral advocacy is persuasively answering the questions. For those of us who are not truly brilliant—and likely even for those who are -there is only one way to effectively answer questions from the bench, and that is to know what they are going to be in advance. This does not require prescience, but diligence and understanding. If you know the weaknesses of your case, or those areas that at least appear at first blush to be weaknesses, you can expect questions from the bench regarding them. The best way to understand the trouble spots in your case is to know your opponent's argument at least as well as she does, for the strengths of your opponent's case are undoubtedly the apparent trouble spots in your own.

In the end, to be truly prepared for possible questions requires a mastery of the field of law involved in the case. It is not possible to anticipate questions by learning a very narrow slice of the field of law involved in the case, for it is necessary to know, and the judges will want to know, how the rule you seek, and the result you desire, fits into the scheme of things. You must be able to supply the answer, and you can only do so by understanding the bigger picture into which your case fits. As Judge Silberman has said, often it is necessary to fit "each new case into a broad and complex mosaic."[6] And again, practicing the argument, particularly in the cases of first impression, and fielding questions at the practice session, is an invaluable method of identifying questions that might be asked by the judges or justices, so as to be prepared with cogent answers.

> I was gratified to be able to answer promptly, and I did. I said I didn't know.
>
> *Mark Twain, Life on the Mississippi*

On occasion, despite diligence in preparation, a judge might ask a question to which you do not know the answer. If the question is one to which you should know the answer and do not, your cause is badly harmed, and this error is avoidable by preparation. But sometimes a judge asks a factual question that may not be pertinent to the issues, simply out of curiosity, or for reasons which are unfathomable, and if you do not know the answer it is best to say so. Even if the question involves a matter you should know, it is better to say that you do not know when that is the case.

To Concede Or Not To Concede

> I was with you Mr. Scott—until I heard your argument.
>
> *Old English Judge*

This is the "Kenny Rogers" principle of appellate advocacy—knowing "when to hold 'em, and when to fold 'em." This principle operates from the beginning of appellate advocacy, in the decision whether to appeal at all, but with regard to oral argument what is meant here is that it is important to understand when to make concessions and when to stand fast. Sometimes judges ask hypothetical questions that change the facts of the case at issue so as to ask whether the rule being advocated would obtain under the altered facts. Insisting that it would can be the height of folly; conceding that it would not can concede away the case. Knowing the difference is the art of advocacy, which can come only from a thorough understanding of the larger principles of law surrounding the particular issue being argued. The appellate prosecutor must so understand the case and the law that concessions can be made where appropriate, to avoid the appearance that the principle argued would cause absurd results (or that the prosecutor does not understand what he or she is talking about). But, even where the judges are hostile to the point being made, the appellate prosecutor must sometimes "hold 'em" and stand fast, despite the discomfort which may be caused by the hostility of the panel, or the case either will be damaged or lost.

When To Sit Down

> He draweth out the thread of his verbosity finer than the staple of his argument.
>
> *Shakespeare, Love's Labor Lost*

A very common error in oral argument is not to sit down when done. On innumerable occasions lawyers, clearly having made all the points intended but realizing there is time remaining, feel compelled to continue. This invariably results in random repetition of points previously made, but far less effectively than originally, and detracting greatly even from what *had* been a solid performance. Plan on being concise from the outset, and once the argument has been made, sit down. Not only will the judges appreciate it, but a concise, tight, interesting argument is extremely effective.

A FEW TECHNICAL POINTS

What To Take To The Lectern?

Some advocate taking nothing. For most, this is too daunting a prospect. Anything—an outline, note cards or even a fully written out argument—is permissible, but only so long as the advocate does not read from the written argument, notes or outline. The advocate must address the judges or justices, and refer to any writings only occasionally.

Speech Patterns And Mannerisms

Here, practice arguments are a help. Avoid talking too fast, and avoid mannerisms, such as wild gestures or jingling change in one's pocket, that are off-putting. This does not mean that the advocate's hands must hold the lectern in a death grip. Natural body movement, and gestures that are not odd or dramatic, are certainly appropriate.

Addressing The Court

Call judges "judge" and justices "justice," as neither likes it when the wrong title is employed. Or the matter may be avoided entirely by the use of "your Honor." If you decide to use names, get them right.

Answering Questions

Of course, always answer a question when asked; never tell a judge or justice you'll get to it later. It is possible, however, to give a short answer, and return to the matter in more depth later in the argument. If a full-blown answer is given, and the point was a part of the planned argument, there is no need to repeat the point later. Judges and justices will frequently take the advocate away from his planned order of argument, and adjusting on one's feet is part of the art of advocacy.

Pay Attention To The Appellant's Argument

Respondent (appellee), as appellate prosecutors are for the bulk of their work, can gain clues from the questions asked appellant's counsel. This may tip off what it is the appellate prosecutor should argue, and what can be set to one side. If it is clear that the court is with you on a point from questions to appellant's counsel, then the argument should be adjusted to let that point go. Care must be taken—and one must know their court—so that one can discern when the questions are simply "devil's advocate" questions, rather than a dismissal of the point made by the defense.

CONCLUSION

> That leads me to the subject of the quality of the government's appellate advocacy. Sadly, but surely inevitably, it has declined over the last two decades... Too often, even in important cases, the government lawyer is badly outmatched by the private (including 'public interest') lawyers.
>
> *Hon. Laurence Silberman*

If Judge Silberman is correct, then appellate prosecutors have a task before them, for the trend he discerns must be reversed in order that public justice be done, as the public is entitled to vigorous and effective appellate advocacy. That advocacy, of course, must always be principled. Demonstrating that the more things change, the more they stay the same, Abraham Lincoln in 1850, while advising on the proper practice of law, observed that "There is a vague popular belief that lawyers are necessarily dishonest... the impression is common—almost universal." Lincoln advised resistance: "resolve to be honest at all events; and if, in your own judgment, you cannot be an honest lawyer, resolve to be honest without being a lawyer. Choose some other occupation, rather than one in the choosing of which you do, in advance, consent to be a knave."[7] Appellate prosecutors must always keep in mind that an effective argument is honorable, and an honorable argument, thoroughly research and prepared, is effective.

ENDNOTES

[1] Lincoln, *Speeches and Writings: 1832-1858* (Library of America: 1989), p 245.

[2] Sir Harold Bowden, in *The New Dictionary of Thoughts* (Standard Book: 1977).

[3] Quoted in American Bar Association Journal, March 1994, p. 50. Appellate advocates used to be allotted more time for argument than presently.

[4] *Michigan v Summers*, 452 US 692, 60 L Ed 2d 340, 101 S Ct 2587 (1981).

[5] Though in the United States Supreme Court one may rest assured that the Court is "engaged;" in my first oral argument there, I received in excess of 100 questions in my allotted 30 minutes!

[6] Silberman, "Plain Talk On Appellate Advocacy," see footnote 2.

[7] Lincoln, *Speeches and Writings: 1832-1858* (Library of America: 1989), p 246.

THIRTEEN

TAKING ADVANTAGE OF ORAL ARGUMENT

KAYE G. HEARN
CHIEF JUDGE
SOUTH CAROLINA COURT OF APPEALS
COLUMBIA, SOUTH CAROLINA

I always feel that there should be some comfort derived from any question from the bench. It is clear proof that the inquiring Justice is not asleep.

Robert H. Jackson (1892—1954), Former Solicitor General for the United States

While sitting on the bench with my colleague, Judge Ralph King Anderson, Jr., a seasoned attorney began earnestly arguing his case. Within a minute or so of the attorney's opening remarks, Judge Anderson posed a question to the attorney. During the attorney's response to the question, the attorney referred to Judge Anderson as "Judge King." Ignoring the mistake, Judge Anderson asked a follow-up question, and again, the attorney called Judge Anderson by the wrong name. This time, Judge Anderson flinched a little, and the attorney asked, "What's wrong, Judge King, am I dancing around your question?" "No, counselor," Judge Anderson replied, "You're dancing around my name!" The attorney was immediately horrified and stammered as he tried to get back to his argument. To ease his discomfort, I joked about his faux pas by suggesting he call me "Judge Queen" for the rest of the argument. The attorney laughed, but was still mortified, and his oral argument suffered.

The fact is, oral arguments are stressful, even for experienced oral advocates. In this chapter, I hope to help attorneys better prepare for their arguments so when the time comes for them to appear before an appellate court, they can focus on making their argument and responding to questions rather than on keeping their composure. As my prior example illustrates, one of the first lessons to learn is to avoid trying to get too fancy during your argument by calling judges by their individual names. The risk of getting their names wrong is much greater than the small benefit you may gain for being familiar with the court.

And, to answer the question I suspect many readers have already wondered by now, oral arguments really do matter. Of course, that is not to say judges come into the arguments without an opinion. In my court, the judges have already conferenced the case, and often times, we have come to a preliminary consensus on how we believe it ought to be resolved. However, in more instances than I would like to admit, we change our minds after hearing the arguments of the parties. Lawyers truly can win their cases during oral argument.

PREPARING FOR YOUR ARGUMENT

Like any performance, successful oral arguments require thorough preparation. While it is absolutely essential for you to be familiar with the record and the briefs, merely re-reading these materials before your argument is not enough. Rather, you must actively read these materials by imagining you are one of the judges being exposed to the appeal for the first time. As you read, write down any questions that come to mind. Doing this will help you anticipate which areas of your argument are weakest so you can focus on being able to answer tough questions about those issues.

Also, keep in mind that if you are arguing before a court that has discretion when setting cases for oral argument, there is probably some distinction between your case and the precedent cited in the briefs. Thus, you must be familiar with the cases that both you and the opposing party cited so that you will be able to answer questions about the facts of those cases as well as the legal principles they set forth. Before arguing, update your research to make sure none of the cases on which you rely have been overturned. Further, keep abreast of any related opinions that were filed during the interim between the writing of your brief and the day of the arguments.

Adequate preparation requires more than merely reacquainting yourself with the record and trying to anticipate judges' questions. You must also spend some time rehearsing your argument aloud. This is not to say you should have a canned speech ready. In fact, oral arguments that are memorized are rarely effective because judges invariably interrupt an attorney's soliloquy with questions, which either seems to fluster or irritate the performing barrister. Think of oral argument as an opportunity for you to have a conversation with the judges. The goal of the conversation is to communicate key points and to make clear the outcome you seek. To familiarize yourself with this type of forum, talk aloud about your case every opportunity you get. Explain the case to a summer intern. Tell colleagues about your case over lunch. Not only will this make you comfortable with hearing your own voice present the case, the questions your audience poses to you may mirror some of the questions the judges will have as well.

Despite my advice against scripting your argument, it is a good idea to develop a strong introduction and conclusion. Compose an opening that captures the court's attention to your position and a closing that leaves the court with no doubt as to what relief you are seeking. The arguments before the United States Supreme Court in *Bowers v. Hardwick*, 478 U.S. 186 (1986) illustrate effective opening remarks:

> Michael Hobbs (Representing Michael Bowers, the Georgia Attorney General): Mr. Chief Justice, and may it please the Court.
>
> This case presents the question of whether or not there is a fundamental right under the Constitution of the United States to engage in consensual private homosexual sodomy.
>
> It is our position that there is no fundamental right to engage in this conduct and that the state of Georgia should not be required to show a compelling state interest to prohibit this conduct.

There is certainly no textual support for this proposition. And, contrary to the views expressed by the Eleventh Circuit Court of Appeals and the respondent, it is suggested that there is no precedential support in the decisions of this Court for the proposition that there is a fundamental right to engage in sexual relationships outside of the bonds of marriage.

Laurence Tribe (Representing respondent Michael Hardwick): Mr. Chief Justice, and may it please the Court.

This case is about the limits of governmental power. The power that the state of Georgia invoked to arrest Michael Hardwick in the bedroom of his own home is not a power to preserve public decorum. It is not a power to protect children in public or in private. It is not a power to control commerce or to outlaw the infliction of physical harm or to forbid a breach in a state-sanctioned relationship such as marriage or, indeed, to regulate the terms of a state-sanctioned relationship through laws against polygamy or bigamy or incest.

The power invoked here, and I think we must be clear about it, is the power to dictate in the most intimate and, indeed, I must say, embarrassing detail how every adult, married or unmarried, in every bedroom in Georgia will behave in the closest and most intimate personal association with another adult.

Note that neither attorney in *Bowers* began by introducing himself to the court, a common but ineffective practice of many appellate lawyers. Instead, you should dive right into the issue of the case and explain why the trial court's decision should be reversed or upheld. Likewise, when concluding your argument, be sure to tell the court exactly how you want it to rule. A strong beginning and strong finish go a long way to producing a strong oral argument, regardless of what happens in between.

As for organizing the materials you may need during the argument, I encourage you to have a manila folder or small binder that contains all the cases cited in the briefs along with a one or two-page cheat sheet that contains a short summary of each case. Without this system, you may find yourself shuffling through a disorganized pile of papers in order to recall the facts of a case, which I assure you, is very distracting to the court. In addition to organizing your authorities, it is also a good practice to tab the briefs and the record so you can quickly flip to important parts. You may even want to copy key pages of the record so they are immediately accessible during the arguments. As I have touched on before, it is better to have a list of talking points rather than an entire script of your argument. Nothing is more boring or exudes less passion than an advocate who reads his or her argument to the court.

PRESENTING THE ARGUMENT

If you incorporate the above advice into your routine for preparing an oral argument, your stress level on the day of your presentation will be drastically reduced. By remaining calm, you will be able to deliver your argument at a normal pace and be better able to control any distracting, nervous habits you may have, thereby enabling you to present your argument more effectively. While arguing, I suggest you place your hands on the podium to avoid making annoying gestures and to hide any shakiness you may experience during the presentation.

As you deliver your argument, which was carefully honed to address the issues you believed were most important to your case, a judge may ask you a question about an issue different from the one you are arguing. When that happens, abandon (at least for the moment) the argument you were making and answer the judge's question immediately. It is never a good idea to tell the judge that you will get to that point in a minute. The judges' questions clue you in on what area of your argument they want you to focus on, so do not waste your time talking about another issue. Likewise, do not attempt to avoid answering the judge's question by answering a different question. That technique fools no one. Instead, when faced with a difficult question, pause for a moment to digest the question and outline in your mind how to answer it. Then, answer the question, and once the point is made, move on. If you are unsure whether you have addressed a specific question adequately, a good technique is to ask the judge whether your answer was responsive to the question.

You may also face a situation where you are asked a question that you simply do not know the answer to. While your impulse may be to take a crack at the answer a la first year of law school, I assure you, it is better to admit ignorance than to make up an answer.

Sometimes, despite your diligent preparation, you will run out of time before you get to the stellar conclusion you had composed. When this happens, acknowledge that your time has expired and immediately conclude your argument in a sentence or two. Of course, if the judges are peppering you with questions when time expires, continue answering them fully. Once there is a lull in questioning, acknowledge that your time is up and sit down. Asking for additional time is rarely advantageous to your position, unless you have to make a critical point and you can make that point in a sentence. Generally, arguments made after time expires are about as persuasive as points your teacher made in high school after the bell had rung.

Finally, no matter what happens during the argument, always be courteous. Never interrupt a judge during his or her questioning and resist any temptation to disparage the opposing party. Remember, this is your last shot to convince the court of your position, so give your argument to the court rather than lodging attacks at the other side.

ASSESSING YOUR PERFORMANCE

No matter how well prepared and eloquent you are, the judges may ultimately disagree with your position. Do not consider the outcome of the appeal alone as a reflection of your appellate skills. Personally, although I always remember an attorney who does a commendable job on an appeal, I rarely remember whether that attorney actually won the case. Think of it this way: No one remembers how many times Benjamin Cardozo was reversed or how many cases Clarence Darrow lost. Likewise, your success as an appellate advocate will not be driven by your won-loss ratio. Rather, it is your level of preparation, your courtesy, and your enthusiasm for appellate work that earns you a reputation for being an effective oral advocate.

FOURTEEN

DECISION MAKING: CONFERENCING OF CASES

JERRY G. ELLIOTT
JUDGE, KANSAS COURT OF APPEALS
TOPEKA, KANSAS

Courts should not roam the unfenced fields of speculation.

State v. Ameen, 27 Kan. App. 2d 181, 184, 1 P.3d 330 (2000).

This chapter presents the first of two views from the bench concerning how the appellate court conferences. While this chapter presents my view from the Kansas Court of Apperals, the Honorable Nathan Mihara, in the next chapter, examines conferencing from the perspective of the Appellate Court in California.

If you know how your court conferences its cases for decision, you can use that knowledge in framing your oral arguments. After all, oral argument is your opportunity to be a part of that decision making process.

I view the purpose of oral argument to be a teaser: try to grab and hold one or two judges' or justices' attention through conferencing. Try to set the hook floated by your brief. Do that, and you have an advocate to continue your point of view and thus (hopefully) influence the decision.

Most appellate courts conference cases using variations of a couple of themes.

FAST/PROMPT

The panel or court will conference cases promptly and try to reach a tentative vote on the outcome of the appeal and the form or approach of the opinion. (For example, published or unpublished; if we decide issue one a certain way, we need not address some or all of the other issues). Some courts make the writing assignments at this time and some courts make tentative writing assignments at the time the docket is set. For what it's worth, both Kansas appellate courts make tentative writing assignments in advance of argument. On the other hand, the Missouri Court of Appeals, Western District, makes the writing assignments during the conference.

If a consensus vote cannot be reached promptly, the court or panel will reconference as needed, either face to face, or by conference call, or by secure e-mail. It is my understanding the federal circuit courts make frequent use of electronic conferencing if they cannot agree when they are together at arguments.

CONTEMPLATIVE

Some courts will hear arguments for a week and commence conferencing those cases on the Tuesday or Wednesday of the following week. These courts may consider the cases in the order they were argued or by some sort of seniority system if the writing assignment has been made. This method of conferencing makes it much harder for you to grab and hold anyone's attention because it may be a week or two before the court gets around to discussing your case.

But, if you can learn what method of conferencing your court utilizes, at least you can better prepare your oral presentation. And, that knowledge should not be all that hard to ascertain. Most appellate courts have publications or web pages which at least hint at the roadmap used.

For example, the Tenth Circuit conferences cases promptly after a day's arguments.[1] The Kansas Supreme Court normally starts conferences on the Wednesday following argument week.[2] The Kansas Court of Appeals, on the other hand, conferences cases promptly following arguments.[3]

Further, the votes at conferences remain tentative until the panel signs off on the opinion or a concurring or dissenting opinion has been added. If the assigned author ends up in the minority, the author trades a case for writing purposes with another member of the panel. On our court, opinions are circulated for comment to the entire court. We do this as a means of consistency control although we have, on occasion, intentionally filed inconsistent, irreconcilable opinions, in hopes the Supreme Court will take the issue on review (conflict among panel decisions is a stated ground for the granting of a petition for discretionary review).[4]

In addition, our web page has photos and biographies of each judge or justice. Further, the biography pages have links to opinions authored by a given judge or justice. If you can find an opinion by a given judge or justice similar to an important issue in your appeal, you should have a candidate for your special advocate. Use that knowledge. Consider targeting that judge during your oral argument on the assumption that person will remember your argument on the issue.

END NOTES

[1] See Practitioners' Guide for the Tenth Circuit at 66. Available at www.ck10.uscourts.gov. Go to "Rules & Forms" and click on "Practitioners' Guide."

[2] See 2003 Kan. Ct. R. Annot. 70. Also available at www.kscourts.org.

[3] See 2003 Kan. Ct. R. Annot. 83. Also available at www.kscourts.org.

[4] K.S.A. 60-3018(b)(2).

FIFTEEN

JUDICIAL CONFERENCING IN APPELLATE COURTS

NATHAN D. MIHARA
ASSOCIATE JUSTICE, COURT OF APPEALS
SIXTH APPELLATE DISTRICT
SAN JOSE, CALIFORNIA

Where there is much desire to learn, there of necessity will be much arguing, much writing, many opinions; for opinions in good men is but knowledge in the making.

John Milton (1608–1674)

I have always been intrigued with how curious attorneys are about the method and manner of judicial conferencing in our appellate courts. Perhaps it is more than simple curiosity. It occurs to me that the common bond of all attorneys, including those who appear in our courts of review, is a desire to prevail on behalf of their clients. At appellate practice courses one would expect to find out how to improve legal research skills, prepare appellate briefing and argue a case orally before an appellate bench. An underlying consideration throughout however has to do with predictability. That is, what counsel can anticipate a particular court might like to see or not, may have a significant impact on how the appellate practitioner might fashion an appellate argument. Further, there would be the benefit of being able to more accurately gauge the likelihood of success on appeal that might in turn influence whether an attorney advises the client to undertake the appeal at all. An understanding of how appellate justices confer can add information that might be relevant to crafting an appellate argument, whether it is in writing or orally presented.

In California there are one hundred ten appellate justices including seven who serve on our State Supreme Court. The intermediate appellate courts are divided into six appellate districts with three of those districts organized into multiple divisions. Our cases are decided by three-justice panels. After spending over eleven years as an associate justice on the Sixth District Court of Appeal and speaking with countless numbers of justices about how things are done in any one of those judicial districts, I can confidently say that while the methods and frequency of conferencing vary greatly, there are also some constants that are worth discussing.

THE INITIAL CONFERENCE

In the distant past, California justices would routinely research and write their own drafts and final opinions. The courts would hire judicial externs or law clerks, usually those just coming out of law school, to assist the justices by preparing bench memoranda and other research to aid the crafting of the ultimate opinion. These externs would serve a minimum of one year and on occasion two years before leaving for other endeavors. Over time, with the influx of greater numbers of cases to decide with fewer additional resources, came the beginning of what we in California have come to know as the career judicial research attorney. As the title suggests, these are bar certified attorneys who have chosen judicial research and writing as their full time occupation. In some courts their function is not too dissimilar from that of the former judicial externs. They prepare bench memoranda for individual justices. Most judicial research attorneys, however, currently have much more responsibility. They not only prepare occasional memoranda on specific issues, but also in the main are expected to prepare actual draft opinions for purposes of judicial conferencing and oral argument. Most significant is the fact that while the topic here suggests judicial conferencing as only between justices on a given case, the importance of the justice and research attorney conferencing should be apparent.

That fact, at least in California, is significant for several reasons. First, the initial discussions the justice has on any given issue might well be with his or her research attorney. Second, it would not be uncommon for the research attorney to speak not only with the justice but also with other attorneys in his or her chambers and ultimately the attorneys from the chambers of the panel justices on the same case. Further, under certain circumstances and perhaps less frequently depending on internal rules of protocol, there may be situations where justices will converse with the research attorneys of a justice who is on the same case. This latter situation usually only occurs with the knowledge and approval of the research attorney's justice whose input is being sought.

The point of this discussion is to illustrate that in matters of reviewing appellate issues, the number of eyes looking at the cases is greater than three sets. Undoubtedly by the time a case has been calendared for oral argument, three or more research attorneys as well as justices have reviewed the case. The important lesson to the appellate practitioner is that when you are preparing an appellate brief, one is doing so not only for the justices about whom you think you may have some knowledge but also for research attorneys who have made it their life's work and passion to read, dissect and analyze appellate arguments.

While the foregoing scenario may be typical for some appellate courts, in other districts the very first conference on any given appellate case takes place only between the justices themselves. The practice usually involves the setting of a specific day of the week for conferencing. At those conferences the justices will have been expected to review all of the cases to be discussed and to have some tentative thoughts about any problematic issues, the course of the analysis and possible disposition. As one might imagine, this may or may not involve research attorney participation by way of a bench memorandum describing the nature of the issues for the justice prior to the judicial conference itself. I know of at least one division where the justices do not consult with their respective research attorneys until after the initial conference. Once the conference is completed, the attorneys are directed by the justices to prepare research memoranda on difficult or complex issues presented. Thereafter, the authoring justice will personally draft an opinion for circulation to other members of the panel.

ADDITIONAL CONFERENCING PRIOR TO ORAL ARGUMENT

Cases coming through our appellate system vary considerably in complexity, numbers of issues presented, length of record, public interest and originality. All of these factors play a role in determining how difficult a case is to conference and whether and to what extent additional conferencing will be needed prior to oral argument. Because by this time the justices have already met once. Further conferences may be held at a meeting, by email or conference call. Just as cases differ, individual justices do as well. Depending on personal preference, some are more inclined to meet face to face either in scheduled meetings or informally on a random basis. Others may prefer to communicate only by way of memorandum once issues and tentative views have been generally defined.

By the time a case is actually heard at oral argument, it should be apparent that it has been well researched and discussed. In fact it is customary in our court for the presiding justice to advise and perhaps remind counsel just before the commencement of oral argument that the court has read the record and the briefs, and is familiar with the issues and facts in the case. In addition, it should not be surprising that the justices will have a tentative view of the appropriate analysis and disposition of the case before argument begins. While this is no doubt true, what counsel usually are not aware of prior to argument is the extent to which the justices have labored over certain issues and have disagreed with either a draft opinion's logic or reasoning, legal analysis, presentation or disposition. I say "usually" to make a point.

When there is significant disagreement on the panel over the analysis or disposition of a case prior to argument and where the author of the draft has not won a single vote, one typical solution absent further conferencing, is to send out to counsel a request for further or supplemental briefing. Such a request should be read very carefully and taken very seriously. While that should be obvious to all, instances have arisen where the replies received from counsel show little or no regard for either the substance of the request or the significance of it. The importance of receiving such a letter cannot be overstated. In short, it is a "window" for appellate counsel into the world of the judicial conference room and an important clue as to what will or will not satisfy a majority of the court to favor one's arguments and prayer for relief. A case may indeed be won or lost based on the quality and the persuasiveness of the supplemental briefing.

However, even if the justices in conference prior to oral argument reject the supplemental briefing's logic and analysis, counsel nonetheless has a second opportunity to persuade at oral argument. At oral argument counsel is now armed with the knowledge of the critical issues as framed by the justices themselves beforehand in their supplemental briefing letter and should not let the opportunity at argument pass without an attempt to advance the supplemental brief's position in an expanded fashion as may be appropriate.

CONFERENCING AFTER ORAL ARGUMENT

In most courts that I am familiar with, including our State Supreme Court, the justices will confer after oral argument has concluded for that particular session. Those conferences will normally occur shortly after argument while the points of law and legal issues and analysis are still fresh in everyone's mind. Points of view are exchanged and if there is any lingering issue to be resolved another meeting can be scheduled to allow time to reflect and engage in further research. Once modifications have been made by the author and approved by the panel in conference or by simply signing a routing slip, the case is prepared for filing.

Continuing disagreement between judges in certain cases is not unusual, even after an engaging and stimulating oral argument, or perhaps because of it. As noted earlier, it may be that panel members have further questions that need to be addressed by the parties after argument. If such is the case, one might receive another request for supplemental briefing. On receipt of that letter, the same considerations noted above apply here, except that one's appreciation of what is troubling the court might be more refined. Again, counsel has been given special insight into what the justices have been talking about in post-argument conference.

Counsel should take full advantage of it. Hopefully, this final opportunity to convince will be successful. Even if not, counsel can be assured that the argument was at least a topic of conversation—judicially speaking.

SIXTEEN

FIELDING DIFFICULT QUESTIONS FROM THE BENCH

PAUL H. ANDERSON
ASSOCIATE JUSTICE
MINNESOTA SUPREME COURT
ST. PAUL, MINNESOTA

A sudden bold and unexpected question doth many times surprise a man and lay him open.

Sir Francis Bacon (1561 – 1626)

Appellate judges enjoy asking questions. It is our lifeblood. It is how we seek to understand a case, eliminate ambiguity, and test a proposed rule of law. We do not purposely think up difficult questions to put appellate advocates on the spot. Nevertheless, many of our questions are difficult to answer because we are testing or probing in an effort to solve complex legal problems.

Most good appellate advocates welcome difficult questions because they know that these questions allow them to engage in a meaningful dialogue with the court. They know that it is only through such a dialogue that they and the court can jointly explore the nuances of complex legal issues. But not all appellate advocates appreciate difficult questions; many view them as an inevitable burden. Why is there this difference? Generally speaking, it can be characterized as a difference in attitude, anticipation, expectation and preparation. By using the foregoing attributes properly, an advocate is able to significantly change the dynamics of oral argument so that even the most difficult questions are welcome or at least palatable. Fortunately, some principles and practices enable an advocate to successfully field the difficult questions. What follows are a few of these principles.

JOINING THE COURT'S DIALOGUE

The Gift

Every question from an appellate judge should be regarded as a gift, even the most difficult question. Perhaps you may find this concept hard to accept, and, admittedly, it may be a concept more readily endorsed by appellate judges and law professors than it is by appellate attorneys. Nevertheless, if you view these questions as gifts, you can create a positive attitude and become a more effective advocate because you will use the information gleaned from the questions to make a persuasive argument.

The following exchange between two attorneys following successive oral arguments before the same court illustrates this point. As the two attorneys leave the courthouse, the first attorney, exhausted and drained by the experience, complains about the number and complexity of the questions asked by the court. He says how much he dislikes questions and wonders why the court would not just let him present his case as he had planned. The second attorney, who also faced numerous, complex questions, responds by saying that she was energized and pleased by her exchange with the court. She states how much she appreciated the court's questions because they provided her with important insights into what the court was thinking, and, as a result, she was better able to address the court's concerns. She says that she finds it more difficult to deal with a "cold bench" than a "hot bench" because the former is so stingy with its insights. The second attorney has the proper attitude toward questions. If you adopt a similar attitude, it will provide you with an excellent foundation for developing a high level of confidence when responding to even the most difficult question.

Another step in developing a positive attitude that will make the most difficult questions palatable is to understand the objective of oral argument. Simply stated, it is an educational process by which the court seeks additional information to enhance its knowledge about the facts and law of your case. An effective oral argument not only increases the court's understanding, it also provides an opportunity to clear up any possible misunderstanding the court may harbor. The court will seek to obtain this information from you. When you do your job well, you will feel welcome in the courtroom because you are a key participant in the process the court uses to reach the correct outcome.

When you appreciate the court's objective for oral argument, you know that your argument should not be a mere recitation of what was in your brief. The court already has that information. The court is looking for something more and will seek to find it by entering into a dialogue with you. Questions are the fuel that powers this dialogue. How effective you are in establishing this dialogue depends upon how well you answer questions, especially the difficult ones.

Moreover, how you answer questions is essential to establishing your credibility. Never underestimate the importance of establishing and maintaining your credibility. The court wants to engage in an honest, forthright dialogue with you. Once you lose your credibility with the court, expect the dialogue to end because the court will have concluded that you have nothing of merit to bring to the conversation. The credibility of your dialogue with the court will depend upon how well prepared you are and your knowledge of what the court expects of you.

Listen And Respond To The Question Asked

When the court poses a question, you should realize that, for the most part, the court is asking the question because a particular judge or the whole court wants to become more informed about a particular aspect of your case. As previously noted, questions are gifts, so treat them accordingly. Listen carefully to understand what is being asked. Do not interrupt the judge by anticipating what the rest of the question may be. Be patient enough to get the complete question. Then, answer the question and do so directly.

Too often an attorney will say, "I will answer that question shortly." There are many dangers inherent in this response—the most obvious being that you will frustrate the court by not answering its question. By putting off the answer, you pass up the chance to shape the argument when the opportunity is presented or, even worse, you may never get back to the question. Under both scenarios, you have wasted an opportunity to respond to an issue that is on the court's mind. The preferred response is to answer the question even if it means a change in your planned case outline. Always remember that this is a conversation that you have been asked to join, not an opportunity to make a speech. Respond to the question that is asked, but attempt to weave an advocacy argument into your answer.

The Courteous Conversationalist

Because the question is your invitation into the court's discussion, you never want to send a negative, demeaning or hostile message to the court. Your nonverbal communication can be as important as what you say. Be aware that the court will pick up on nonverbal communication such as eye, hand and body movements that can either enhance or interfere with establishing an effective dialogue. If you put both hands firmly on the podium and assume the stance of a middle linebacker, it is a sure sign that you are defensive and that you do not welcome questions, and, if you do get a question, you will throw it right back at the court. Instead, you should assume a more relaxed stance that sends the message that you want to engage in a constructive dialogue.

Some nonverbal communication can be as explicit and disparaging as verbal communication. On one occasion, an experienced criminal appellate attorney appeared before a panel that was composed of a number of recently-appointed appellate judges. Two of the judges asked questions that were basic and general in nature, but nevertheless were relevant to the case. The words the attorney used to answer the questions were appropriate, but through his impatient tone and body language, the attorney sent a very disparaging message to the court. It was as if he had made a sign of exasperation and said "What do I have to do, teach you a course in Criminal Law 101?" The panel noted and commented on the attorney's conduct and found it offensive. You should be aware that nonverbal communication can take you to and beyond the bounds of proper conduct. Consider, as the attorney here did not, that sometimes the most basic questions are the most difficult to answer, but their basic nature does not render them irrelevant or unreasonable. Finally, as an advocate, remember there are no stupid questions by the court.

PREPARATION AND ANTICIPATION

How The Court Prepares

As in most endeavors, preparation is the key to success. The properly prepared attorney is able to take potentially difficult questions and turn them into responses that work to his client's advantage. Part of your preparation should be to understand how the court prepares for oral argument. This information will provide insight into what the court expects from you and the questions that will be asked. Chapters 14 and 15 provide detailed insights into how some appellate court justices/judges conference and communicate with each other.

Some courts only engage in a limited review of a case before oral argument and use oral argument to form a general outline of the case. Only after oral argument will these courts delve deeply into the record and case law. While this approach is limited to a minority of courts, if you know that this is how these courts prepare, it will enable you to anticipate the type of questions that they are likely to ask. Most questions may be broad in scope and oriented toward establishing a background on what the case is about. Be prepared to answer these questions in a way that will focus the court's attention on the issue that is at the heart of your case. On the other hand, always be ready for the follow-up question that has a laser sharp focus on an essential aspect of the key issue. Here, lack of anticipation or being lulled into a sense of complacency can turn a helpful question into a difficult question.

Most courts, especially those where review is discretionary, will have engaged in an extensive review of your case before argument. The court will have reviewed the lower court's decision, read the briefs, examined the relevant parts of the record, and will have had the benefit of a bench memo prepared by either a law clerk or staff attorney. If done properly, the bench memo will not merely repeat what is in the briefs; rather, it will be a value-added document. The value the bench memo adds is an independent arms-length analysis of your case. It will include a comparison of the facts in the record with the facts as briefed by you and opposing counsel. It will also include a detailed review of the case law cited and an independent analysis of whether this case law supports the position you want the court to adopt. A good bench memo will point out to the court omissions and improper or inconsistent factual representations. It will also disclose improper or ill-founded citations to case law. At oral argument, you will most likely face well-informed judges prepared with questions geared to reveal any flaws in your case theory.

The foregoing judicial preparation will lead to a number of difficult questions if you are not as well or better prepared than the court. Your preparation should include submitting a brief that is correct about both the facts and the law. Candor with respect to the record is crucial. Avoid the temptation to believe that when there is a voluminous record, you can omit some essential fact or slip some facts by the court. Never improperly "massage" or "play" with the facts. An appellate court has little patience with such endeavors and they can quickly undermine your credibility as an advocate.

No question is more difficult or embarrassing to field than a question from the court that points out an error in your factual statement or in your legal citations. You can avoid these difficult questions by doing your homework. If, however, you do make a mistake that leads to such a question, do not compound that mistake by attempting to dodge the question or further mislead the court. Do not squander your credibility; own up to your error, cut your losses, and move on.

At this point, it is important to add a note of caution. As important as it is to own up to a mistake, it is just as important not to concede too much. Conceding too much can turn a difficult question into a disaster. Insufficient preparation or an inability to master the issue at the heart of your case can lead you to concede more than is necessary. Be mindful that there are often nuances to facts that should and must be pointed out to the court, misunderstandings that need to be clarified, and subtle aspects of the prior case law that distinguish it from your case. An imprudent concession in response to a question can turn out to be the death knell for your position when the court conferences your case.

How The Court Views Your Case—The Three Categories

How does the court view your case? To achieve a reasonable degree of comfort when confronted with difficult questions, you should understand how the court views your case. Broadly speaking, there are three categories of cases that come before appellate courts, and the category of case often drives the types of questions that the court will ask.

Cases in the first category often cause judges to wonder why the case is before them on appeal. In such cases, the facts have been sorted out and are unalterable given the record and the standard of review. In addition, the applicable law is generally well-established. In essence, an appellate court can or should do nothing but affirm. At oral argument, the court may have only a few questions or perhaps none at all. If you are the appellant, you will likely be asked, either explicitly or implicitly, "Why are you here taking up our valuable time?" You should have a good answer for this question or you should not have appealed the case in the first place. As Elihu Root said: "About half the practice of a decent lawyer consists of telling would-be clients that they are damned fools and should stop."[1]

The second category of cases is more challenging. The facts are established by the record below and the applicable law is also well-established; but, for some reason, the attorneys or the lower court have not sorted out the facts or the law. Here, the appellate court must dig into the facts and the law, sort them out, and then juxtapose them. Essentially, the court involves itself in a sophisticated version of the game where you put the square peg in the square hole and the round peg in the round hole. Once this sorting is completed, the result comes into focus and the outcome is obvious.

The court's opinion in this second category of cases will necessarily devote significant time to sorting out the facts and articulating the law so that everyone can see how the connected dots make the outcome readily apparent. Oral argument will be part of the process. Therefore, you are likely to get probing questions that attempt to sort out both the facts and the law. You will be able to answer such questions if you have done some sorting out of your own between the time the lower court rendered its decision and oral argument. If not, you face the prospect that the court will confront you with questions about a case or line of cases that you have overlooked and, with some chagrin, you will be left wondering "Why didn't I think of that?"

The third category of cases also may need some sorting out of both the facts and the law, but even when this sorting is done, the answer still is not clear. There may be a statute with ambiguous language or the parties may even dispute whether the language is ambiguous in the first place. When the statute is ambiguous, the ultimate outcome may turn on a question of policy and intent. If so, legislative history may be an important part of any analysis. These cases are the most arduous cases for appellate courts to decide and they are usually the most closely contested.

Oral argument in the third category of cases can be intense when the court seeks to sharpen its focus. Questions can be probing, wide-ranging, and sometimes peppered with hypothetical questions, some of which will be well-constructed, while others may be lengthy and lacking in focus. You may get philosophical questions on policy which ask you to state what is good and bad public policy. Think about the policy that both supports and undermines your position so you can answer the court's questions in a manner that makes the strongest statement in support of your position.

You should be prepared to respond quickly, clearly, and candidly to questions about the general rule of law you advocate and the implications of applying that rule not only to your case, but also to other cases in the future. Ordinarily, an attorney should have no difficulty answering a rule of law question, but if you fail to anticipate such a question, your answer will most likely be inadequate. You should never let yourself be put into a position where "Counsel, what is your proposed rule of law?" becomes a difficult question to answer.

In all three case categories, there is no sure way of eliminating all potentially difficult questions. But if you take the time to sort out what general category your case fits into, you will have taken a major step toward anticipating difficult questions and turning them to your advantage.

ANSWERING PARTICULAR TYPES OF QUESTIONS

The Premature Question

Some may say that there is no such thing as a premature question from an appellate court. Support for this proposition comes from courts that have a reputation for asking the first question even before you get to the podium and introduce yourself. Nonetheless, a good appellate advocate is always prepared for what can be characterized as the premature question. This question usually is directed at a key issue in your case and is asked by an anxious judge before you get a chance to establish the essential factual or legal foundation of your case. It is the timing of this question that makes it so difficult.

You must answer the premature question. It will do you no good to dodge it. When you respond, do so in a manner that weaves crucial contextual background into your answer. Anticipation and preparation can be of help here because a well-designed strategy can get you through this difficult stage in your argument.

Be prepared to have your answer to the premature question interrupted by a second judge. Anticipate that just as you are about to reach an important aspect of your legal argument, you may be interrupted by a second question from another judge who is seeking more context and thus directs her question at a specific factual aspect of the case. This second question may soon be followed by a third question from another judge who wants you to elaborate on yet another factual aspect of your case.

At this stage, you may feel like a juggler with too many balls in the air. Keep your sense of balance and attempt to answer each question, even if it means reordering them. After you have dealt with the factual questions, do not be afraid to indicate to the court that you now wish to complete your answer to the initial question, but this time you can do so with more contextual background.

Often, a premature question from the court will cause your dialogue with the court to become disjointed and incomplete. Be prepared to return to the key issue later in your argument when you can give a more complete answer with the proper context. This approach requires preparation, focus and discipline. Remember, many arguments fail because the attorney does not give the best argument on a key issue. Sometimes a member of the court is willing to help you out by bringing you back to your key point. Be prepared to recognize this help when it arrives.

The Softball Question

Some questions will arrive neatly gift wrapped and with friendly overtones. Therefore, it is a mistake to assume that all questions are adversarial or even hostile. Appellate judges ask you questions to inform themselves and their colleagues, or sometimes to convey a specific message to their colleagues. In some aspects, oral argument is really the first stage of the court's conference. Sometimes a judge knows the answer to her question, but wants you to provide the answer for the rest of the court. The judge knows that the proper answer will take a potentially contentious issue off the table at the court's conference or cut the foundation out from under a position that one of the other judges is inclined to adopt. Most likely the questioning judge favors your side of the issue, but realizes that you did not get an opportunity to fully answer an earlier question that is essential to your argument. The judge is providing you with a second chance to get it right—take it.

You must anticipate friendly questions and recognize them when they come. When preparing yourself to respond to these questions, you should see yourself as a batter in the batter's box with your intellect, skills, and knowledge of the facts and law as your bat. The judge asking the question is the pitcher. But instead of throwing a sharp breaking curve low and away, the judge sends a pitch over the center of the plate with enough speed to contain substance, but slow enough so that with a proper swing, you can hit it out of the ballpark. If you are unprepared or too defensive, you may leave your bat on your shoulder, thus letting a marvelous opportunity go by. The well-prepared advocate will recognize the pitch, swing and hit it out of the ballpark. Seek to touch all the bases with your own response and persuade the court on the point the questioning judge wants to make. Sometimes you may swing, but only get some wood on the ball. Then, you get the equivalent of a base hit. You partially make your point, but not as well as you could or should have. Nevertheless, you did recognize the softball question and got a piece of it. The essence of this analogy is to always look for this type of question and be prepared to swing for the fences. Never leave the bat on your shoulder.

The Stupid Question

There are no stupid questions from an appellate court. If you accept this proposition at face value, it will help you to abide by a cardinal rule of appellate advocacy: never disparage the court. Remember, the court holds the power over the outcome of your case. Your response when faced with what you believe to be an uninformed or stupid question can probably best be described by a comment of Judge John Rawls who said "[Y]ou can think it, but you better not say it." *Vandenberghe v. Poole,* 163 S0.2d 51 (1964). You are well advised to never respond to any question as though it is meritless.

However, you may confront inarticulate questions that by their nature are difficult or nearly impossible to answer. When confronted with such a question, take a deep breath, pause a moment, and do your best. Never show your frustration or take out your frustrations on a court you are trying to persuade.

If you cannot answer the question, seek clarification or admit your dilemma to the court. Alternatively, carefully rephrase the question in a manner that you believe is consistent with its intent, and then answer that question. When you take this approach, always do so in a respectful manner so as not to offend the court. Always attempt to keep the dialogue going and never burn your bridges with the court. Remember there is always the chance the court's question was neither stupid nor inarticulate, but rather it just went over your head because the court is exploring an aspect of the case you had not considered. Be willing to accept responsibility for any failure to receive the court's message clearly. Most courts are willing to accept an inquiry about whether you are correctly understanding its questions. Failure to follow these principles can turn a question into a hostile relationship with the court.

The Nasty Hypothetical Question

Hypothetical questions always rank near or at the top of the list when appellate attorneys talk about difficult questions. From an appellate advocate's point of view, they are fraught with potential problems. They can lead to unwarranted concessions and an ill-conceived response can destroy the credibility of your argument. Often, hypotheticals are not a model of clarity; frequently they are long and can be convoluted. But they are an essential tool for appellate courts.

Understandably, you want to win the case for your client, and you have developed a theory that you hope will achieve this goal. Part of your theory is a rule of law that you want the court to adopt. But appreciate the fact that the court is less concerned about whether you win or lose than it is about adopting a solid rule of law that has broad integrity and makes good policy. The court will test the integrity of your proposed rule of law by using a hypothetical. Therefore, anticipate and plan for tough hypothetical questions.

When you get a hypothetical question, answer it. If you do not, you most likely will offend the court and implicitly concede that it is not answerable in a manner favorable to your cause. As stated earlier, do not concede too much and be prepared to distinguish your case when presented with an unfavorable hypothetical. The court is testing a possible holding and is exploring the outer edges of your proposal. If you push your argument too far, a hypothetical can box you in so that you wind up with no place to go. Once again, proper preparation and an understanding of the court's objective will reduce the difficulty of responding to the court's hypothetical questions.

Opposing Counsel's Questions

As the respondent (appellee) and as an appellant anticipating rebuttal, you must listen carefully when the court questions opposing counsel. These questions frequently provide clues that will reduce the difficulty of the subsequent questions you will face. A court frequently will ask the same question of both sides. When the court asks the same question the second time, it anticipates that you will not only answer its question but also address the points raised by opposing counsel. To be forewarned is to be forearmed, so take advantage of this early warning device.

Sometimes the court will ask a question of one side when its real intent is to get an answer from the other side. In these circumstances, the court anticipates what the first party's response will be, but knows that the other party's answer may well determine the case's outcome. In essence, the court is giving a heads-up to be prepared to answer a key question. The court is seeking a well-thought-out answer and is willing to signal its intent. Listen for, hear, and act on these signals when they are given. They offer the opportunity to answer the toughest question to your advantage.

A FINAL WORD ABOUT PREPARATION

At oral argument, you can reduce the number of difficult questions and even eliminate them if you anticipate and prepare properly. As you prepare, visualize the court walking down a hallway lined with many doors and behind one of the doors is the route to the correct outcome. To be properly prepared for oral argument, you need to walk down this same hallway. You need to explore what is behind each door.

Often what is behind one door appears promising, but further exploration reveals that there is yet another promising door to be opened. Only after opening a number of doors does it become apparent that the route taken does not lead to a good outcome and may even lead to a bad rule of law. As a result, you must backtrack to the original hallway and continue to explore each set of doors until you ultimately come to a route that leads you to the right result. The court will explore the same hallway in search of its conclusions and holding. If you hope to assist the court as it explores its alternatives, you must explore that hallway before the court does. Your exploration will put you in a position to discover the answers to the questions the court is likely to ask. Thus you can with comfort, confidence, and ease answer the court's most difficult questions about what route it should take.

ENDNOTES

[1] *The Quotable Lawyer*, p. 189, edited by David Shroyer and Elizabeth Frost. New England Publishing Associates, Inc. (1986).

SEVENTEEN

INSPIRATIONAL WORDS FOR THE APPELLATE PROSECUTOR

DONALD J. ZELENKA
ASSISTANT DEPUTY ATTORNEY GENERAL
SOUTH CAROLINA ATTORNEY GENERAL'S OFFICE
COLUMBIA, SOUTH CAROLINA

What an advocate gives to a case is himself; he can bring to the bar only what is within him. A part written for him will never be convincing.

Justice Robert H. Jackson, formerly Solicitor General of the United States[1]

As a prosecutor and an appellate advocate, I treasure each day I arrive at the office. We have been given, by the grace of our governmental employers, an extraordinary job with extraordinary responsibility—to represent the law-abiding people of our state, to defend our system of justice, and to ensure that the victims of the crimes which occur within our jurisdictions are zealously represented. I am often asked why I have continued in my work as an appellate advocate in a prosecutor's office rather than enter private practice. In being asked a similar question, Kevin W. Lyons, the State's Attorney for Peoria, Illinois said it best: "Why do we do what we do? Because they did what they did!"

As appellate advocates, we know that each case we handle can and often will not only be reviewed by appellate courts within our state, but frequently will be reviewed by federal courts and the United States Supreme Court. We know that the path of the litigation is in our hands and we must not falter. The trial prosecutors, whose prior hard work can come undone if we are not diligent, have consented to have us handle their cases through the duration of the litigation. The court system relies upon us to be accurate and fair in our presentations. The courts demand that we present honest, candid and persuasive arguments.[2] Each of us must retain civility toward opposing counsel and remember that their role is only to be an advocate for their client. We must also recognize that defense counsel does not share personal responsibility in the criminal acts of their clients, but are duty bound to provide them with what our great Constitution demands—zealous and effective assistance of counsel. Our role as prosecutors, however, is much higher—to be a minister of justice and the representative of the sovereign.

Within the public office we hold, appellate prosecutors are regularly faced with increasing budget problems and an ever-increasing criminal appellate caseload. Somewhat remarkably in hindsight, in my quarter-century as an appellate prosecutor, the issues raised have not become any easier or routine to handle. Any attempt to rely upon former responses have not addressed my need as an advocate. Appellate advocates are constrained to the information and evidence within the transcripts, but we are called upon to breathe life into these printed words so the appellate court can understand the purpose and impact of what occurred in the original trial setting. Yet, unlike the excitement of the trial, we are constrained to the solitary life of reading hundreds of pages of the record within the narrow confines of our office.

In preparation of the brief and ultimate preparation for an oral argument, each of our offices necessarily expects us to carry out our responsibilities as a soloist, rather than as part of a quartet, and trusts us to carry out our duties professionally. As a young lawyer, this can be a thrilling experience. While our colleagues from law school who are in their mega-size law firms may still be seeking to question their first witness in a deposition, the young government advocate is presenting the position of the people. As an appellate advocate, we responsibly stand alone when the court asks us questions about our case and about our policy.[3]

Often, appellate prosecutors are faced with opposing lawyers from large law firms from both within the state or national law firms. Do not let yourself be intimidated by their presence. Chief Justice William Rehnquist provides encouragement that should be heeded:

> Our Court is naturally more likely to be influenced by a good brief than a bad brief, and by a good oral argument than by a bad oral argument. But I think I can state categorically that it is not the least bit likely to be influenced by the fact that the brief is signed, or the oral argument is made, by a lawyer who practices in Washington rather than somewhere else. Nor is it the least bit likely to be influenced by the fact that the brief is signed, or the oral argument made, by a well-known lawyer from a large firm anywhere in the country as opposed to a little-known lawyer from a small firm anywhere in the country.[4]

Throughout this book, appellate practitioners, experts and jurists provide the reader with unique insight on how to prepare the individual brief and the individual argument. However, a rewarding career as an appellate prosecutor may be the course chosen either by you or by your agency for you. The purpose of this chapter is to try to continue both the motivation and the inspiration many of us have felt in this career as an appellate lawyer in the public sector by sharing with you some advice, information and a variety of sources to inspire a life in the law, particularly as an appellate advocate. .

The most important resource any lawyer will find is the lawyer's broad personal development. Prudent advice was given in the following letter from Supreme Court Justice Felix Frankfurter to an aspiring law student:

> My dear Paul,
>
> No one can be a truly competent lawyer unless he is a cultivated man. If I were you, I would forget about any technical preparation for the law. The best way to prepare for the law is to come to the study of the law as a well-read person. Thus

alone can one acquire the capacity to use the English language on paper and in speech with the habits of clear thinking which only a truly liberal education can give. No less important for a lawyer is the cultivation of the imaginative faculties by reading poetry, seeing great paintings, in the original, or in the easily available reproductions, and listening to great music. Stock your mind with the deposit of much good reading, and widen and deepen your feelings by experiencing vicariously as much as possible the wonderful mysteries of the universe and forget all about your future career.

With good wishes,

Sincerely yours,

Felix Frankfurter[5]

Daniel Webster, when asked as to the amount of time he spent preparing one of his memorable arguments is said to have replied that his whole life was given to its preparation.[6]

Justice Robert Jackson similarly wrote:

The effective advocate will not let mastery of a specialty foreclose the catholicity of interest essential to the rounded life and balanced judgment. He will draw inspiration not alone from the literature of the law, but from the classics, history, the essay, the drama, and poetry as well. It is one of the delights and intellectual rewards of the legal profession that it lays under tribute every science and every art. The advocate will read and reread the majestic efforts of leaders of his profession on important occasions, and linger over their manner of handling challenging subjects. He will stock the arsenal of his mind with tested dialectical weapons. He will master the short Saxon word that pierces the mind like a spear and the simple figure that lights the understanding. He will never drive the judge to his dictionary. He will rejoice in the strength of the mother tongue as found in the King James version of the Bible, and in the power of the terse and flashing phrase of a Kipling or a Churchill.[7]

To be successful, every lawyer must take care of themselves emotionally and mentally. As appellate prosecutors, we have chosen the career path which exposes us to the worst of society's ills. A typical day will have the lawyer dealing with unspeakable cruelty and crimes by a defendant and undeserved tragedy in the victims' lives. We may be asked to advise a suffering crime victim of the reality that the case may have to be retried due to an error which had nothing to do with guilt or innocence. Our daily review of the violence in life today may test our emotional resolve. Years of successful advocacy may be ended by the last court to hear the matter due to intervening changes in the law.

The appellate advocate must prepare for this difficult task by balancing his or her life with the advice given by Justices Frankfurter and Jackson to take care of your own mental and physical state. Closure must be sought in many different ways to avoid appellate burn out. This advice, if heeded, will serve you well.

I have been given the great opportunity to appear before the United States Supreme Court on a number of occasions. In addition to the moot court critiques, visits to the Court to view other oral arguments and the dutiful solitary preparation this opportunity demands, I have one tradition that always returns my focus to this unique role. Before each argument, I visit the National Archives and view the United States Constitution. While there, I pay particular attention to the portion of it which concerns the precise issue being presented in the Court. Each time I have done this, the importance of our role as prosecutors, as ministers of justice and as guardians of the great tradition of the law solemnly hits home. This brief diversion has always inspired me to continue in this role with its great opportunity in public service.

Similar opportunities may exist in your area in preparation of your own appeals. It may be a routine matter, such as reflection upon your own state constitution and bill of rights or ensuring that contact has been made with the victims or trial prosecutors. In cases where narrow technical issues are raised, I try to view as much of the relevant trial evidence as possible to have an awareness of the crime itself, not just the issues involved.

In discussing what inspiration drives other appellate practitioners, many have expressed that the fear of not doing well and appearing unprepared is the main motivation for their own advocacy. This fear drives their preparation for the case. "Great men, great nations, have not been boasters and buffoons, but perceivers of the terror of life…"[8] However, "knowledge is the antidote to fear."[9] Stated another way, "to be conscious that you are ignorant is a great step toward knowledge."[10] Turn this fear into a benefit by using it to focus on the preparation. Remember to focus on the case, not on the fear.

Each of us can recall our own nervousness during the early stage of our careers when presentations were made to the courts. I can recall that I feared that my neck and spine were noticeably shaking as I approached the podium. Be advised that with experience, this nervousness goes away. As a crutch to focus my attention to the case at hand, when I rise for an argument, I will always button my coat. This brings my attention to the solemnity of the proceedings, as well as my role as the state's advocate. This also reminds me to be calm, particularly after an opposing advocate may have been baiting me personally during the argument. While an advocate should always address issues raised by the opposition, with appropriate preparation, it should not change the focus of your prepared remarks. As Justice Jackson stated "The most persuasive quality in the advocate is professional sincerity."[11]

In addressing the advocacy of lawyers, Chief Justice Warren Burger stated:

> …A truly qualified advocate—like every genuine professional—resembles a seamless garment, in the sense that legal knowledge, forensic skills, professional ethics, courtroom etiquette and manners are blended in the total person. There are some lawyers who scoff at the idea that manners and etiquette form any part of the necessary equipment of the courtroom advocate. Yet if one were to undertake the list of the truly great advocates of the past 100 years, I suggest he would find a common denominator: they were all intensely individualistic but each was a lawyer for whom courtroom manners were a key weapon in his arsenal. Whether engaged in the destruction of adverse witnesses or undermining damaging evidence or in final argument, the performance was characterized by coolness, poise, and graphic clarity, without shouting, without baiting witnesses, opponents or the judge.[12]

If you perform well and lose or if the appellate court utters an opinion difficult to accept, consider this advice:

> It cannot be too strongly emphasized that the manner in which [the judge] performs his function in the judicial process depends almost entirely upon the condition of these tools when you, the lawyer, place them in his hands, for you originate the suit, conceive and give form to the action, prepare the testimony, conduct the hearing, and present to the Bench for adoption the proper solution of the questions raised. The resulting fabric of justice is so much your responsibility that it has been said a Bench can be no stronger than its Bar.[13]

After you have completed this appellate advocacy experience, you should review your written and oral presentation with this assessment:

> If you give reasonable attention to these sundry observations you will make an effective presentation in written or oral word of the points you deem favorable to your client. If you do that you will have brought home an understanding of your side of the cause and have performed your full duty. After that the decision rests in hands beyond your control. You will then have done your damnedest—angels can do no more.[14]

LITERATURE ABOUT APPELLATE LAWYERS

Following the advice of Justice Frankfurter, a well-rounded background is a necessary tool for a lawyer. Contrary to popular belief among the Bar, there are books about appellate lawyers, judges and former law clerks that can provide inspiration for a life in the law.

- *Lawyers Lawyer: The Life of John W. Davis* by William H. Harbaugh Univ Press of Virginia (1990) Paperback—648 pages, $22.50. This biography of one of the primary Supreme Court litigators reveals an interesting public life involving an appellate lawyer and power-broker.

- *The Tenth Justice: The Solicitor General and the Rule of Law* by Lincoln Caplan. This book is an interesting account of the Solicitor General's Office in prior administrations, the power it yields, and policy decisions it makes on whether and what to present to the Court.
- *The Majesty of the Law: Reflections of a Supreme Court Justice* by Justice Sandra Day O'Connor and Craig Joyce. Her unique observation on the Court, the development of the law and the emerging role of women in the law is presented in this volume.
- *On Appeal: Courts, Lawyering, and Judging* by Frank M. Coffin, R.S. Means Company (1996) Paperback (373 pages) $10.00. In the *Kirkus Review*, the book was described as an erudite, informative, and witty tour of American appellate courts, those courts that review the legal decisions of trial courts and give litigants a second chance at justice. He presents the historical background and present characteristics of the often sharply contrasting English common law and European civil law models. Coffin lays out at length the distinctive elements of American appellate practice. He contrasts the federal and state appellate systems, pointing out both the dominance of state appellate courts and the problems that dog them. The author treats virtually every other aspect of appellate advocacy and judgeship from clerks to conferencing the opinions with recommendations on brief writing and oral argument.
- *Closed Chambers; The Rise, Fall, and Future of the Modern Supreme Court* by Edward Lazarus, Penguin Books Paperback (1999) 592 pages $15.95. An inside look at the most secretive institution in the American government—the Supreme Court by Justice Blackmum's former law clerk. This book received a significant amount of press because of the tell-all manner of the author's style and his characterization of the power of the law clerk. It also described an internal war within the institution between conservative and liberal law clerks for the soul of the court.

UNDERSTANDING THE LAW

There are also written works which may provide the advocate with a better understanding of the law as we grow in our experiences.

- *The Bill of Rights: Creation and Reconstruction* by Akhil Reed Amar, Yale Univ Pr Hardcover—352 pages (1998) List Price: $30.00. Amar's landmark work invites citizens to a deeper understanding of their Bill of Rights and sets the basic terms of debate about it for modern lawyers, jurists, and historians for years to come. In our continuing battles over freedom of religion and expression, arms bearing, privacy and states rights, Amar concludes that we must hearken to both the Founding Fathers who created the Bill and their sons and daughters who reconstructed it.
- *The Constitution and Criminal Procedure: First Principles* by Akhil Reed Amar, Yale Univ Pr; (1998) Paperback, 288 pages $16.00. Akhil Amar examines the role of search warrants, the status of the exclusionary rule, self-incrimination theory and practice, and a host of Sixth Amendment trial-related rights. He challenges the utility of the exclusionary rule in his treatise.

CLASSICS—A SELECTED FEW

Shakespeare and other classics will inspire us.

- *The Breath of an Unfee'd Lawyer: Shakespeare on Lawyers and the Law* by William Shakespeare, Jerry Warshaw (Illustrator), Edward J. Bander (Editor) Catbird Press (Paperback) (1996) ($13.95). A little Shakespeare goes a long way. Et tu Brute.'
- Camus, Albert. *The Fall.* New York: Vintage, 1956.
- Dickens, Charles, *Bleak House.* New York: Oxford University Press, 1998.
- Kafka, Franz. *The Trial.* Definitive ed. New York: Schocken Books, 1995.

- Melville, Herman, *Billy Budd.* New York: Oxford University Press, 1998.
- Shakespeare, William. *The Merchant of Venice.* New York: Pocket Books, 1992.

LEGAL THRILLERS WITH AN APPELLATE NEXUS

In the fictional genre of legal thrillers, appellate courts and appellate lawyers can provide a worthy backdrop to a relaxing story. Here are some by some of today's leading writers.

- *Murder in the Supreme Court* by Margaret Truman (Fawcett Books 1985). This a fictional mystery involving the murder of an employee of the United States Supreme Court.
- *The Simple Truth* by David Baldacci (Warner Books 1999). This fictional work involves a law clerk to a Supreme Court justice who becomes involved in investigating the case of a convicted murderer whose case is before the court.
- *The Tenth Justice* by Brad Meltzer (Warner Books 1998). A Supreme Court law clerk inadvertently reveals the result of a pending case with significant economic impact.
- *Reversible Errors* by Scott Turow (Warner Books 2003). A corporate lawyer becomes appointed in death penalty habeas appeal. Against a fictional background, this story follows the course of death penalty litigation and investigation.
- *Pelican Brief* by John Grisham (Dell Publishing Company 1993). Two Supreme Court justices are assassinated. A brief prepared by a law student leads to cover-ups and Washington intrigue.
- *Final Appeal* by Lisa Scottoline (Harper Torch 2000). A federal appeals court law clerk assigned to a death penalty appeal leads to revelations of deception and corruption within the appellate court.

- *Protect and Defend* by Richard North Patterson (Ballantine Books 2001). The Chief Justice collapses and dies at the inauguration of a new President. The appointments process gets boggled into the mix of an intriguing abortion and right to life issue.
- *After Dark* by Philip Margolin (Bantam Books 1996). A recent law clerk to an Oregon Supreme Court justice enters the job market. The story involves revenge of a recently released convicted murderer, a death penalty trial, in addition to inferences of judicial and political corruption present in many legal thrillers.

APPELLATE LAW RELATED MOVIES

Although appellate law is not always the most exciting part of our practice, some movies have been made about appellate courts and lawyers. Some of these are inspirational, but some are just entertainment.

- *First Monday in October* (1981). A comedy about the first woman appointed to the Supreme Court, a conservative, and her colleague, a crusty but benign liberal judge. Though based on a Broadway hit, it ended up foreshadowing the real-life appointment of Sandra Day O'Connor, which occurred at about the time the film was released. The characters, however, bear no resemblance to the Court or its members. Walter Matthau's infamous quote "wilderness of free association" was his description for the Court.
- *Amistad* (1997). A drama about the 1839 slave uprising on a slave ship and trial for murder and piracy, which went to the Supreme Court.
- *Judgment at Nuremberg* (1961). This is a strong dramatization of the Nazi war crime trials. Supreme Court Justice Robert Jackson was involved in the trial.
- *The Magnificent Yankee* (1951). The groundbreaking legal giant Oliver Wendell Holmes arrives in Washington in 1902 and in

the next thirty years become the "Great Dissenter." This movie portrays more of his domestic life than his legal career.

- *Separate But Equal* (1991). A made for television movie. It traces the development leading to the decision in *Brown v. Board of Education* by the United States Supreme Court.
- *To Kill a Mockingbird* (1962). Although not related to appellate law, any inspirational movie list must include this classic. This is a drama of Harper Lee's novel telling the story of Atticus Finch and his daughter Scout and how Atticus defends a black man wrongfully charged with rape in a racially-biased environment.
- *Breaker Morant* (1980). As with *To Kill a Mockingbird*, this is an example of another film which inspires all lawyers. An excellent Australian court-martial movie set in the time of the Boer War. Three Australian lieutenants are treated as scapegoats when prosecuted for executing prisoners of war.

CONCLUSION

An appellate prosecutor toils in the law library in the never-ending tasks of research and transcript review, must remember that "work is not punishment. It is (the advocate's) reward and (the advocate's) strength and (the advocate's) pleasure."[15] We have the opportunity to have our names associated with opinions, both great and small, as we change and protect the fabric of legal history. Not only are we ministers of justice, we are forever associated with the opinions which arise from our work which will shape the course of trial and the law in the future. If the maxim that "the best use of life is to spend it for something that outlasts life"[16] is correct, the life and work of an appellate prosecutor is one to be cherished.

ENDNOTES

[1] Robert H. Jackson, *Advocacy Before the United States Supreme Court*, 37 Cornell Law Quar. 1 (1951).

[2] "Clarity, candor, and simplicity are of the essence. One unfortunate consequence of our present system of legal education is that young lawyers find ingenious arguments especially appealing. But these are poison in most appellate courts. A judge approaches an argument that appears to be ingenious with instinctive suspicion; it gives the distinct impression of being merely verbal. If the legal argument appears to flow naturally from well-settled legal principles, you have satisfied in the best possible way the intellectual element of your appeal". Breitel, Gates, Knapp, Marshall, Pollack, Rifkind & Steinberg, *Counsel on Appeal*, 130 (McGraw-Hill, Inc. 1968).

[3] Supreme Court Justice Robert H. Jackson declared: "When he rises to speak at the bar, the advocate stands intellectually naked and alone. Habits of thought and speech cannot be borrowed like garments for the event. What an advocate gives to a case is himself; he can bring to the bar only what is within him. A part written for him will never be convincing." Robert H. Jackson, *Advocacy Before the United States Supreme Court*, 37 Cornell Law Quar. 1 (1951).

[4] William Rehnquist, *The Supreme Court – How It Was, How It Is* (Knopf 2001).

[5] Maxwell Taylor Kennedy, *Make Gentle The Life of This World: The Vision of Robert F. Kennedy* (New York, Broadway Books 1999), p. 109.

[6] Robert H. Jackson, *Advocacy Before the United States Supreme Court*, 37 Cornell Law Quar. 1 (1951).

[7] *Id.*

[8] Ralph Waldo Emerson, *Essays, Second Series* (1841).

[9] Ralph Waldo Emerson, *Society and Solitude*, "Courage" (1870).

[10] Benjamin Disraeli, *Sybil* (1845).

[11] E. Barrett Prettyman, Jr., "Supreme Court Advocacy: Random Thoughts in a Day of Time Restrictions," 4 *Litigation* 16 (Winter 1978), p. 19.

[12] Warren E. Burger, Lecture, Fordham University Law School, reported in the *Los Angeles Times, December 28, 1973,* reprinted in *The Quotable Lawyer* 194 (1986) (D. Schrager and E. Frost eds.).

[13] Fournet, "The Effective Presentation of a Case to the Supreme Court in Brief and in Argument," 3 La.B.J. 95, 97 (Jan. 1956).

[14] Carswell, "The Briefing and Argument of an Appeal," 16 Brooklyn L. Rev. 147, 159 (1950).

[15] George Sand, *Mauprat* (1837).

[16] William James, *The Will to Believe and Other Essays in Popular Philosophy*, Cambridge, MA and London: Harvard University Press, 1979, originally published 1897.

ACKNOWLEDGEMENTS

Authors of chapters for this book have worked together before as faculty members for Appellate Advocacy courses at the National Advocacy Center in Columbia, South Carolina. Appellate prosecutors in attorney general's and prosecutor's offices from across the nation benefited from these courses. As the saying goes, "You learn more teaching than you ever do as a student." This certainly was true of the Appellate courses where the attendees taught not only each other but also the faculty members. This work is a product of their dedication to appellate advocacy and to their vigorous participation in the courses. We also want to acknowledge the contributions of our colleagues, the other faculty members who taught at the Appellate courses.

The National District Attorneys Association, under the leadership of Thomas Charron, then the Director of Education at the National Advocacy Center, and the National College of District Attorneys, headed by Dean Robert Fertitta, deserve credit for sponsoring those valuable Appellate courses. NDAA staff members Abney Wallace, Rhonda Grant, Sheila Casserley and Jan Bilton ensured the smooth running of the courses. Margaret Fent served as course director for some of those

Appellate courses, and she has our thanks for her contributions to and enthusiasm for the Appellate courses. We wish her well now that she has returned to the courtroom as a prosecutor.

Seattle University Law School supported the creation of this book; special thanks to Professor Marilyn Berger. The editor wishes to extend thanks to those at the Law School who provided technical assistance for the text layout: Jasmina Kostich, Secretary, Adjunct Professors; James Cooper, Director of Instructional Technology and Multimedia Services, and Lori Lamb, Senior Administrative Assistant, Legal Writing Program,

As always, I am indebted to my wife Nancy for her support and guidance and particularly for proof reading this book.

Ronald H. Clark
Editor

THE AUTHORS

JUSTICE PAUL H. ANDERSON is an Associate Justice of the Minnesota Supreme Court. A graduate of Macalester College and the University of Minnesota Law School, Justice Anderson was a Vista Volunteer, Special Assistant Attorney General for the State of Minnesota, and was in the private practice of law for twenty-nine years before being appointed Chief Judge of the Minnesota Court of Appeals in 1992. He was appointed to the Minnesota Supreme Court in 1994 and was reelected in 1996. Justice Anderson is a contributing author for the National College of District Attorneys' book on professional responsibility, entitled *Doing Justice: A Prosecutor's Guide to Ethics and Civil Liability.*

TIMOTHY A. BAUGHMAN is the Chief of Research, Training, and Appeals for the Wayne County Prosecutor's Office, Detroit, Michigan. Mr. Baughman received his B.A. from Albion College and his J.D. from Wayne State University Law School. Mr. Baughman has been an assistant prosecuting attorney for over 29 years, and he has appeared four times in the United States Supreme Court, each with a successful result, and has supervised the briefing and argument of four other cases in that Court.

He has briefed and argued over 60 cases in the Michigan Supreme Court, and is the author of two books and various articles on criminal law and criminal procedure. He has lectured for the Michigan Judicial Institute, the State Bar of Michigan, the National College of District Attorneys, and for prosecuting attorneys associations of various states throughout the country.

J. KIRK BROWN is Nebraska's first Solicitor General. Prior to that appointment he was the first Criminal Bureau Chief and Chief of the Criminal Appellate Section of the Nebraska Department of Justice for over 12 years, and directly responsible for Nebraska's death penalty litigation. Mr. Brown has successfully briefed three cases on the merits before the Supreme Court of the United States, and has been counsel of record in 238 other appellate cases in the state and federal courts. He has received a Supreme Court of the United States, Best Brief Award from the National Association of Attorneys General, and an Appellate Advocacy Award from the Association of Government Attorneys in Capital Litigation. Mr. Brown has lectured nationally on the subjects of the death penalty, appellate advocacy, federal habeas corpus and correctional law, and has served on the faculty of the National College of District Attorneys Appellate Advocacy Course. He is a graduate of the University of Nebraska, College of Law.

HILARY L. BRUNELL earned her law degree at George Washington University. She became an Assistant Prosecutor in the Essex County Prosecutor's Office in Newark, New Jersey in 1979, and Deputy Director of the Appellate Section in 1983. Two years later, she placed her career on hold to raise two children. She returned to the Essex Office in 1998 to the position of Deputy First Assistant Prosecutor and was named Executive Assistant Prosecutor in 1999. Through out her career, she has specialized in appellate practice, and in 1994 received the Regional Vice-President's award for excellence in appellate advocacy from the Association of Government Attorneys for Capital Litigation. She has appeared many times before the state Supreme Court of New Jersey, she frequently lectures on topics ranging from appellate advocacy to trial evidence.

JUDGE JERRY G. ELLIOTT was appointed to the Kansas Court of Appeals in 1987. He received a liberal arts degree from Kansas University in 1958 and his LLB with distinction, from Kansas University in 1964, where he was Order of the Coif and editor-in-chief of the Kansas Law Review. Following a clerkship with a federal trial judge, he practiced with the Foulston Siefkin firm in Wichita, Kansas, where he spent about 70% of his time in civil appellate practice. He has been a frequent faculty member for the Appellate Advocacy program at the NAC.

PROFESSOR JAMES FLANAGAN is the Oliver Ellsworth Professor of Federal Practice at the University of South Carolina School of Law. He graduated from the University of Notre Dame and the University of Pennsylvania Law School. He served as an Assistant United States Attorney for the District of Columbia in the Felony Trial and Appellate Divisions from 1970–74. After practicing as a trial lawyer in Chicago he joined the faculty in 1979 and concentrates on courses for the trial advocate including civil procedure, criminal procedure and evidence in state and federal courts. He is an experienced trial and appellate advocate and has appeared in state and federal courts in the District of Columbia, Illinois and South Carolina, and has served as advisor to several moot court teams at the law school. He is currently a member of the United States District Court Rules Advisory Council, the South Carolina Circuit Court Rules Committee and is the Chair, Magistrate Advisory Committee.

ROBERT M. FOSTER is a Supervising Deputy Attorney General in his 30th year with the Appeals, Writs and Trials (Criminal) Section of the California Attorney General's Office in San Diego, California. He is a graduate of Hastings College of the Law, San Francisco. He has briefed, argued, and won, two cases at the United States Supreme Court (including *California v. Acevedo*) and over 15 cases at the California Supreme Court. His main area of practice is in the state appellate courts where he has handled over 1,500 appeals. He has orally argued over 400 cases in the state appellate courts. He has over 80 published decisions. He is the author of the chapters on writing respondent's briefs in Purver and Taylor's *Handling Criminal Appeals* published by Bancroft Whitney. He was the founder and first director of the San Diego National Wine Competition. He regularly judges commercial wine competitions in California, Missouri, and Virginia

JUDGE KAYE HEARN has served as a member of the South Carolina Court of Appeals since her election in 1995 and has been chief judge since 1999. She received her B.A. degree from Bethany College in 1972, and her Juris Doctor degree from the University of South Carolina School of Law in 1977. She received an L.L.M. degree from the University of Virginia's Graduate Program for Judges in May 1998. Judge Hearn began her legal career by serving as a law clerk to the Honorable J.B. Ness, Associate Justice of the South Carolina Supreme Court. From there, she became a trial attorney with the firm of Stevens, Stevens, Thomas, Hearn, and Hearn. In 1986, she was elected to the family court bench where she remained until her election to the court of appeals.

JUDGE BARBARA P. HERVEY is a judge on the Texas Court of Criminal Appeals. She received her undergraduate degree from the University of North Carolina at Greensboro and her law degree from St. Mary's University School of Law. She was in private practice for five years following her graduation from law school and then joined the Bexar County Criminal District Attorney's office in San Antonio, Texas. She served as an assistant district attorney in the appellate section for sixteen years. She has taught at the National College of District Attorneys and is a frequent lecturer throughout Texas. She is an adjunct professor, teaching Texas Criminal Procedure, at St. Mary's University in the fall. She received the Rosewood Gavel Award for judicial service from St. Mary's in 2003 and has recently been elected to the American Law Institute.

JUDGE ROBERT J. HUMPHREYS received his undergraduate degree from Washington & Lee University in 1972 and a *Juris Doctor* degree in 1976 from Widener University Law School. He has been a judge of the Court of Appeals of Virginia since 2000 and also serves on the Virginia Sentencing Commission. Before assuming the bench, he spent 22 years as a prosecutor including election to three terms as Commonwealth's Attorney in Virginia Beach, Virginia and as a Special Assistant United States Attorney for the Eastern District of Virginia. He is a past president of the Virginia Association of Commonwealth's Attorneys and past Chairman of the Commonwealth's Attorneys Services Council. He has also served on the Virginia State Crime Commission. In 1996, he received the *Robert F. Horan, Jr. Award for Outstanding Service* to Virginia prosecutors. Judge Humphreys has lectured extensively throughout the country on the subjects of legal ethics, technology crime, and both trial and appellate advocacy to prosecutor's associations, bar associations and governmental organizations including the National Science Foundation, the National District Attorneys Association and the United States Department of Justice. He is also a longtime faculty member of the National Advocacy Center and the National College of District Attorneys and is a recipient of that organization's *Stephen Von Reisen Lecturer of Merit* Award. He served as an adjunct professor of law at the University of Dayton School of Law from 1998 through 2000 and since 2001 serves as an adjunct professor of law at the Regent University Law School.

JUDGE MICHAEL E. KEASLER is a judge on the Texas Court of Criminal Appeals. He received his undergraduate and law degrees from the University of Texas. He was a prosecutor in Dallas County for twelve years, tried over four hundred jury trials, and was the senior felony chief prosecutor in the Career Criminal Division. He then served as district judge in Dallas for seventeen years. He served as Chair of the State Bar of Texas Judicial Section and the ABA State Trial Judges' Ethics Committee. He was also dean of judicial education in Texas. He has taught at the National Judicial College since 1992 and was the April, 2002, Robert H. Jackson Lecturer. He is also a member of the American Law Institute and teaches ethics and statutory construction nationally.

JUSTICE NATHAN D. MIHARA is a 1972 graduate of the University of Washington, in Seattle, Washington, with a B.A. degree in economics and a 1975 graduate of Hastings College of the Law in San Francisco, California. He had a private law practice in Menlo Park until he joined the California State Attorney General's Office. From 1977 to 1985 he was a Deputy Attorney General in the San Francisco office where he represented the State of California in criminal trials and appeals including death penalty cases before the California Supreme Court. Justice Mihara served as a trial court judge; first on the Santa Clara County Municipal Court beginning in 1985 until he was elevated to the Santa Clara County Superior Court in 1988. In 1993, he was appointed to the State Court of Appeal as an Associate Justice in the Sixth Appellate District. Justice Mihara has been a faculty member of the California Center for Judicial

Education and Research and the California Appellate Courts Institute. He currently serves on numerous judicial committees including the Judicial Council's Appellate Advisory Committee and is chair of the Appellate Legislative Subcommittee.

JUDGE CHARLES E. MOYLAN, JR. is a retired Judge sitting on the Maryland Court of Special Appeals, where he has served for over three decades. Prior to that he was the State's Attorney for Baltimore City, and, during his tenure there, he was named the Outstanding Prosecutor by the National District Attorneys Association. Judge Moylan has lectured to prosecutorial and judicial groups in all 50 states on topics including, among other: search and seizure; trial tactics; double jeopardy; confrontation; the history of homicide law; presumptions, inferences, burdens of proof and due process of law, and the history of the law of evidence. He has been an Adjunct Faculty of Law at both University of Maryland and University of Baltimore Schools of Law. Judge Moylan authored numerous books and law review articles including: *Criminal Homicide Law* (Published by MICPEL (2002)); *Maryland's Consolidated Theft Law and Unauthorized Use* (Published by MICPEL (2001)), and *The Right of the People to be Secure: An Examination of the Fourth Amendment* (Published by the National College of District Attorneys, Houston, Texas (1976))(Revised Second Edition 1979)). He received his B.A. from Johns Hopkins University and graduated from University of Maryland Law School.

J. FREDERIC VOROS, JR. is Chief of the Appeals Division of the Utah Attorney General's Office. He supervises a division of 16 attorneys who handle all felony appeals statewide, as well as all state and federal post-conviction matters. He has handled hundreds of appeals, including criminal, civil, and agency matters. Prior to joining the Division in 1991, he maintained an active civil litigation practice, including handling appeals for clients ranging from the First National Bank of Boston to a convicted murderer. He is past chair of the Appellate Practice Section of the Utah State Bar and a frequent lecturer on criminal and appellate law. Mr. Voros teaches appellate advocacy as an Adjunct Professor of Law at the S.J. Quinney College of Law, University of Utah. A native of San Luis Obispo, California, Mr. Voros graduated from Brigham Young University

(1975) and its J. Reuben Clark Law School (1978). He clerked for Utah Supreme Court Justice Dallin H. Oaks 1981–82.

DONALD J. ZELENKA is an Assistant Deputy Attorney General and Chief of Capital and Collateral Litigation in the South Carolina Attorney General's Office in Columbia, South Carolina. He is a graduate of The Ohio State University and the University of South Carolina School of Law. Mr. Zelenka has been with the Attorney General's Office since 1979, handling criminal appeals and federal habeas corpus actions. Currently, he supervises all murder appeals, federal habeas corpus action and capital litigation. Mr. Zelenka has personally argued five cases before the United States Supreme Court, over 100 cases in the United States Court of Appeals for the Fourth Circuit, and numerous cases in the state appellate courts. He has also tried a number of murder cases in the trial court. He is a past president of the Association of Government Attorneys in Capital Litigation, and a former chairperson of the South Carolina Bar Criminal Law Section. Mr. Zelenka has received several honors including the "Silver Scales Of Justice" Award for outstanding public service for victims of crime by the South Carolina Victim Assistance Network and the Judge William J. Schafer Award from the Association of Government Attorneys in Capital Litigation for excellence in capital litigation. Mr. Zelenka is also a frequent lecturer on appellate practice in state and national courses.

Printed in the United States
By Bookmasters